1,000,000 Books

are available to read at

---◇---

www.ForgottenBooks.com

---◇---

Read online
Download PDF
Purchase in print

ISBN 978-1-330-53646-9
PIBN 10075362

This book is a reproduction of an important historical work. Forgotten Books uses
state-of-the-art technology to digitally reconstruct the work, preserving the original format
whilst repairing imperfections present in the aged copy. In rare cases, an imperfection in
the original, such as a blemish or missing page, may be replicated in our edition. We do,
however, repair the vast majority of imperfections successfully; any imperfections that
remain are intentionally left to preserve the state of such historical works.

Forgotten Books is a registered trademark of FB &c Ltd.
Copyright © 2018 FB &c Ltd.
FB &c Ltd, Dalton House, 60 Windsor Avenue, London, SW19 2RR.
Company number 08720141. Registered in England and Wales.

For support please visit www.forgottenbooks.com

1 MONTH OF
FREE
READING

at

www.ForgottenBooks.com

By purchasing this book you are eligible for one month membership to ForgottenBooks.com, giving you unlimited access to our entire collection of over 1,000,000 titles via our web site and mobile apps.

To claim your free month visit:

www.forgottenbooks.com/free75362

* Offer is valid for 45 days from date of purchase. Terms and conditions apply.

English
Français
Deutsche
Italiano
Español
Português

www.forgottenbooks.com

Mythology Photography **Fiction**
Fishing Christianity **Art** Cooking
Essays Buddhism Freemasonry
Medicine **Biology** Music **Ancient**
Egypt Evolution Carpentry Physics
Dance Geology **Mathematics** Fitness
Shakespeare **Folklore** Yoga Marketing
Confidence Immortality Biographies
Poetry **Psychology** Witchcraft
Electronics Chemistry History **Law**
Accounting **Philosophy** Anthropology
Alchemy Drama Quantum Mechanics
Atheism Sexual Health **Ancient History**
Entrepreneurship Languages Sport
Paleontology Needlework Islam
Metaphysics Investment Archaeology
Parenting Statistics Criminology
Motivational

Wm. Coles, Watford.

WILLIAM CALLOW, R.W.S., F.R.G.S.

AT THE AGE OF EIGHTY-SIX.

WILLIAM CALLOW

R.W.S., F.R.G.S.

AN AUTOBIOGRAPHY

EDITED BY

H. M. CUNDALL, I.S.O., F.S.A.

LONDON

ADAM AND CHARLES BLACK

1908

DEDICATED

TO

MY DEAR WIFE LOUIE

IN RECOGNITION OF

HER DEVOTION AND LOVING CARE OF ME

DURING OUR TWENTY-FOUR YEARS

OF HAPPY MARRIED LIFE

YPRES.

PREFACE

IT was originally intended that I should assist Mr. William Callow in writing his autobiography, but it was decreed otherwise.

Fortunately for the purpose of this book Mr. Callow wrote minute diaries whilst on his early walking tours to the Pyrenees, in Switzerland, and in Italy, and for a long period he kept notes of the principal events of his life. These notes, on account of his failing sight, Mrs. Callow read out to him during the long winter's evenings, and owing to his wonderful memory he was enabled to recall the various episodes in his career, which Mrs. Callow carefully wrote down as he recounted

vii

them. She had barely completed her task before Mr. Callow passed away in the early part of the present year. All that I have done has been to put the events of the long and eventful life of this noted water-colour painter into a chronological and readable form, and without the very cordial assistance given to me by his widow my portion of the work would have been in vain.

Hearty thanks are due to the various owners of his paintings, who have been so good as to allow them to be reproduced for the purpose of illustrating this book. The water-colour painting of the Interior of St. Mary's Church, Richmond, Yorkshire, was kindly lent by Miss E. Ponsonby M'Ghee for reproduction. This lady has since presented it to the Royal Society of Painters in Water-Colours, in order that it may be added to their collection of works of deceased members of the Society, as a mark of her great appreciation of the genius of William Callow.

The small illustrations inserted in the text have all been selected from the large number of pencil drawings and sketch-books which were in the artist's possession at the time of his death.

H. M. CUNDALL.

October 1908.

MONT ST. MICHEL.

CONTENTS

WILLIAM CALLOW

CHAPTER VI

ST. VALERY EN CAUX.

LIST OF ILLUSTRATIONS

IN COLOUR

IN BLACK AND WHITE

DRESDEN.

In Memoriam

To few it is vouchsafed the privilege of leading such a long and eventful life as that enjoyed by William Callow. He lived in the reigns of five Sovereigns. He commenced early in the nineteenth century, when only a boy of eleven years of age, to gain his own livelihood by practising the rudiments of art, and continued his artistic career uninterruptedly until well into the beginning of the present century.

William Callow was descended from an old eastern counties family, originally called de Calewe, and his grandfather, John Callow, born in 1750, was an artist engaged in the decoration of porcelain at the Lowestoft factory.

There was about William Callow a peculiar charm of naturalness, which made him to be beloved even by those who were brought into contact with him only once. He was possessed of a serenely beautiful countenance and a fine and imposing presence, accompanied by great courtliness of manner. This latter quality was doubtless to a certain extent inborn in his nature, and it was brought to a condition almost of perfection during the long period of his attachment to the Court of King Louis Philippe and other Royal personages with whom he was brought in contact both in Paris and Potsdam. His habits of life were of the simplest character, and in Buckinghamshire, where for so many years he made his home, he was greatly beloved by all who knew him.

He possessed a remarkably strong physique, and during his last years it was his custom to walk five or more miles each morning, unaided by a stick, which he vehemently rejected. Even until the very day on which he was attacked by his fatal illness he had enjoyed this daily exercise.

His memory was wonderfully clear up to the

last, and he was able to entertain his friends by recounting many interesting events in his early life with the greatest fluency. As a conversationalist he had few equals. His presence at a dinner-party was always sufficient to ensure its success by his never-ending source of anecdotes and witticisms, which entertained the whole party and kept them in a state of merriment. In fact, it is said that in the neighbourhood of Great Missenden no hostess settled the date of her dinner-party until she had assured herself that Mr. Callow could be present. With the exception of a failing sight, which unfortunately deprived him of the power of continuing to depict the scenes which he had visited, coupled with a slight deafness, few would have guessed that he had entered his ninety-sixth year.

He had an intense love for good music. During his early days in Paris he frequently visited the Opera, where he heard all the greatest artistes of the time, and later, by his first marriage, he became connected with some of the finest musicians in this country.

With his gentle nature he greatly resented any cruelty to dumb creatures, and the brutal treatment of horses, which he frequently witnessed in Italy, filled him with horror. He had an intense love for birds, and in his own garden they became so accustomed to him and so tame that they would often perch on an arm of the chair in which he was seated.

Owing to the rough cobble-stones with which the streets of Paris were paved when William Callow first resided there, he acquired a habit of looking on the ground whilst walking, in order to see where to tread. The result was that he was frequently so fortunate as to find money and valuable articles on the ground. In Paris he once picked up a gold watch and chain for which he was never able to find an owner, but the most important incident of this nature occurred about six years previous to his death. Whilst walking along the parade of a well-known seaside resort he espied two small linen bags attached together by a string. On examining the contents one was found to contain a pocket-book in which were stocks and shares amounting to about three thousand pounds as well as several bank-notes, whilst in the other was some gold coins and several valuable rings set with diamonds and other precious stones. He soon discovered the owner of the lost property; it turned out to be a lady, who explained that she had tied the bags round her waist under her skirt for safety.

William Callow received his earliest instruction in drawing from Newton and Theodore Fielding, and gained some knowledge in the application of water-colours from his friend Charles Bentley, who was a fellow-pupil with him at the Fieldings; but Callow considered his great love for painting architectural subjects to have been acquired by his association with John Shotter Boys whilst they were together in Paris. Callow, like Boys, did not belong to the severe class of architectural draughtsmen who minutely depict every detail of ornament, but street scenes, with picturesque buildings and overhanging houses, usually composed the chief features of his compositions, in which effective disposition of light and shade and masses of colour, forming harmonious contrasts, display a more conspicuous part than local exactness. He also acquired a taste for making watercolour paintings of shipping and seascapes. Charles Bentley became well known as a marine painter, and as he and Callow were always fast friends and made many sketching tours together, the former may very probably have influenced Callow's art in this direction.

During his first long walking tour to the Pyrenees in 1836 Callow made many of his sketches carefully in water-colours, but later he chiefly confined himself to his pencil whilst travelling both abroad and in England. Besides filling numerous sketch-books he was in the habit of making careful pencil drawings. These he always kept, and at the time of his death he had accumulated many hundreds of them. It was his practice to execute all his finished paintings in his studio from these pencil drawings. He had such a wonderful memory for colour that he was enabled to depict the scenes which he had sketched years ago with only the aid of his black and white drawings.

He never commenced one of his finished paintings, not even to sketch it in with his pencil, until he saw the whole subject complete in his mind and he knew exactly the way in which he would treat it. He chiefly worked by inspiration. He was known to look through hundreds of sketches and feel he could not do justice to any of them. Afterwards an inspiration would suddenly come to him, and he would set to work in earnest, invariably completing the painting before commencing another subject. He was a wonderful draughtsman, and his hand was so steady that he never required, even in his most elaborate subjects, to remove a line once he had drawn it.

William Callow took up oil painting shortly before the year 1850, and contributed pictures to the British Institution and Royal Academy, continuing to do so almost annually to the former till its close in 1867, and to the latter until 1876, when he shortly afterwards relinquished oil painting and confined himself to water-colours.

With regard to his water-colour paintings it is surprising how little his style changed all through his long life. He first learnt his broad manner of painting in Paris seventy years ago, and the works executed during the present century have the same free handling of pure water-colour. He strictly adhered to the early principles of the Old Water-Colour Society forbidding the use of body-colour. He preferred a hard, non-absorbent paper, and generally used Whatman paper, which he did not tone either by staining or washing with any colour. There was no preparatory work; he commenced with whatever local tint he required. The drawing was then washed with pure water and allowed to dry before the next tint was added, the hard edges being softened with a brush and water.

His earliest paintings were exhibited in France, and he was awarded medals at Cambrai in 1836 and 1839, at Boulogne-sur-Mer in 1837, and at Rouen in 1839 and 1840, whilst at the Paris Salon he had the honour of receiving a gold medal in 1840 for a water-colour painting, "A View of Richmond," which attracted the attention of the Royal Family of France, and was the means of his first being brought into association with them.

He was the last of the fashionable drawing-masters. Whilst he was in Paris he taught the children of King Louis Philippe and many of the French nobility, and on his taking up his residence in England he continued to give lessons in drawing until a comparatively recent period to innumerable pupils. Amongst them may be mentioned two Viceroys of India, the late Earl of Northbrook and the Marquis of Dufferin and Ava, besides many judges and military officers. Amongst his lady students were the late Baroness Meyer de Rothschild, Lady Antony de Rothschild, and Lady Amherst of Hackney and her six daughters.

William Callow was greatly beloved by his fellow-members of the Royal Water-Colour

Society, and to show their great appreciation of his loyalty to the Society they presented him with an illuminated address on the occasion of his ninetieth birthday, and subsequently it was the custom of many of them to pay annual visits, both on his birthday and New Year's Day, to him at his home at Great Missenden.

In 1907 he was persuaded to have an exhibition of his paintings at the Leicester Galleries. It proved to be a great success, and William Callow received many hundreds of letters of congratulations both from friends and strangers in all parts of the country. He himself visited the Exhibition on the 26th October of that year, which proved to be the last visit he ever made to London or elsewhere. Early in the present year he was attacked with influenza, succeeded by bronchitis, from which he never recovered, and died on 20th February, at Great Missenden, where he had resided for more than fifty years, and where he was greatly beloved and revered. His nobility of character and charming personality endeared him to all who had the privilege of knowing him. Of his private generosity none will ever know, but he was generous to a fault, especially in cases of suffering. He was buried in Great Missenden Churchyard, and the funeral service was attended by the President, Vice-President, and many other of his fellow-members of the Royal Water-Colour Society, as well as by numerous residents anxious to pay a last token of respect to "the grand old man," as they loved to call him.

WILLIAM CALLOW

CHAPTER I

BOYHOOD

I HAVE always retained pleasing recollections of my native town, the old historical borough of Greenwich. In early days I used to revisit it with my father in a Thames wherry, and at a later date, by a more rapid means of progression, in a steamboat. I was born on the 28th of July 1812, and was one of a family of four; my two sisters and my brother John, who was ten years my junior, all have predeceased me. When I was only one year old my father, who was at the time employed at Greenwich, received an appointment as manager of works for alterations and improvements in the barracks at Norman Cross on the Great North Road near Stilton, where the French prisoners were confined during the Napoleonic wars. Here, I was told, prisoners used to nurse and make much of me; it was a strange coincidence that I should become in later life so intimately associated with France and her countrymen. After peace was proclaimed in 1815, my father's appointment terminated, and he with his family returned to Greenwich. During our residence there the allied sovereigns of Europe met in Greenwich Park and I was taken to see them, but I have no recollection of the event. My earliest reminiscences were travelling in the basket of a coach and being put down at the Ship Inn at Charing Cross, when my parents came to London and permanently settled there. I well remember, when eight years of age, being taken to see the funeral procession of Queen Caroline, the wife of King George IV.; the cortège was obliged to pass along Tottenham Court Road instead of the New Road, owing to the latter route being blocked by the authorities. Of my school days I have but a dim recollection. Unlike most boys I was more disposed towards quiet reading or drawing than boisterous games; in fact, I never saw cricket, football or any other game played at that period of my life. A love for drawing rapidly developed at this early age, and I eagerly drew everything which attracted my attention; my father wisely encouraged it by providing me with prints to copy.

In 1823 an event occurred which was destined to decide my future career. Mr. Theodore Fielding, an elder brother of Copley Fielding, required a boy to assist him in colouring prints and in engraving in aquatint. My father applied for the position for me and I was ultimately engaged. I commenced work at 26 Newman Street, Oxford Street, and my hours were from 8 A.M. till 6 P.M. At first I found the time terribly long, and the postman's bell at five o'clock, when he came to collect the letters, was always a welcome signal that a day's work was nearing its close. In those days the postage fee was paid to the postman, or, as more often was the case, letters were despatched unpaid. I was occupied in this position for two years, and my evenings were spent in receiving lessons from a schoolmaster near our home in Camden Town, whilst my spare moments were devoted to drawing. It was during the time I was in Newman Street that I first saw the beautiful water-colour drawings of Copley Fielding, who forwarded them from Brighton, where he lived, to be despatched to the Old Water-Colour Society. Mr. Copley Fielding gave me a ticket for the Exhibition, and it was a proud day for me when I went to see Fielding's works hung on the walls with those of John Varley, Samuel Prout, Peter De Wint, David Cox and others, little thinking that my own productions would ever occupy a similar position.

In 1825 Theodore Fielding removed to Kentish Town, and I was articled to him as a pupil for eight years for instruction in water-colour drawing and aquatint engraving. At that period it was all open fields between Camden Town and Kentish Town, and as I returned home in the evening the watchman from his box used to bid me good-night as I passed. There were two other pupils, Charles Bentley and John Edge. This was a very happy period of my life. These pupils both assisted me in acquiring the methods employed for my work. To the former I owe much, as he encouraged me to paint; in fact, he gave me my first painting lesson, and assisted me in every way to bring out my natural talents.

In 1827 Theodore Fielding, having some time previously been appointed Professor at Addiscombe College, found it necessary to remove to Croydon to be near to his work, and Bentley and Edge, having finished their time, left to start life on their own account. I was no longer required, and returned to the office at Newman Street, which was then being managed by another brother, Thales Fielding. Here I continued engraving, but all my spare moments at home were occupied at water-colour painting, rising early and working late in order to do so. I used to show my drawings to Copley Fielding, who gave me great encouragement and kind advice. At last when I had seven finished drawings I determined to try and sell them. I set off to a dealer's at the bottom of Holborn Hill, considering all the way how much I should ask for them, and thinking how rich I should be on my return. I felt rather nervous on entering the shop, but on showing the drawings to the dealer he agreed to my price, viz. one guinea for the lot. He would not, however, give me any money, but offered painting materials in exchange, which I took, being delighted at having, as I thought, made such a good bargain.

In 1829 my father was superintending some repairs at Windsor Castle for King George IV., which gave me an opportunity of seeing all over it. I was delighted with everything I saw, and made a few small sketches there. Early in the same year I visited Theodore Fielding at his residence in Combe Lane, Croydon, to assist him in some work. At that time, previous to the advent of the railway, Croydon was quite a country town, and the passing through of the Brighton fast coach was the chief event of the day. This was my first visit to the country, and I vividly remember the strolls along the quiet lanes where the nightingales sang, the lovely walks across the fields to Combe Hurst, not then enclosed, and sitting on the hill to watch the sun go down, sometimes sketching, but always with a feeling of peaceful enjoyment. I was enraptured, for I had never known before what it was to enjoy real country life. I returned to London on the 25th June, and an event now occurred which was the turning-point in my life. In the following month, before I had completed my seventeenth year, Mr. Ostervald, a Swiss, called on Mr. Thales Fielding, and stated that he required some one to go to Paris to assist him in making engravings for a work on Switzerland. Mr. Fielding asked me whether I would like to go. To this proposal I at once consented without hesitation, and promised to be ready within a week. On reaching home in the evening my parents were much surprised to hear the news, but nevertheless everything was made ready so that I was able to start at the appointed time.

DIETZ.

CHAPTER II

IN PARIS

On the 16th July 1829 I left home alone for a
foreign country. I knew scarcely a word of French,
and all I had to assist me were a few questions
written on a sheet of paper, without any answers.
My father and one of my sisters saw me off from
Charing Cross at eight o'clock in the evening by the
mail coach to Dover. The coach passed through
Gravesend and Rochester, stopping at the latter
place for refreshments in the real old coaching

days' style, and after travelling all night it reached
Canterbury at six o'clock the next morning, when I
was put inside the coach by the guard, and slept
soundly until I was awoke by the blowing of the
horn as the coach entered Dover, and on looking
out of the window beheld the sea for the first
time. I went to see Mr. Thales Fielding, who
was staying at Dover, and after having partaken
of a good breakfast I proceeded on board the
steamer, lying in the harbour near the old jetty,
which still exists. Although delighted at being
on the sea, I was so tired that I fell asleep almost
immediately after the steamer started, and did
not wake up until three hours afterwards, just as
the steamer was entering Calais harbour. Some
friendly passengers assisted me in securing a seat,
first on the English coach to Boulogne, and afterwards on the French diligence, which reached
Paris in forty-eight hours. On descending from
the diligence I hired a porter to carry my baggage
to Mr. Ostervald's, to whom I had a letter of
introduction, but on arrival at his house I found
that he was away from Paris; so with the help
of my written phrases I explained to the servant
that I would leave my luggage and call again
the next morning. I then retraced my steps to

ENTRANCE TO THE HARBOUR,

(*Size* 10 × 14½ *inches*)

the diligence office in order to find out where
Hôtel Dauphin was situated, but after trying in
vain to understand the words, gestures and signs
as to the route, I hired a cabriolet, in which the
passenger sat beside the driver, it being the only
vehicle on hire in the streets of Paris in those
days. On arrival at the hotel I paid the driver
by holding out a handful of silver that he might
take his fare. Whether he cheated me I never
knew. I had only been in Paris three days when
I was asked if I could lend some money for a short
time. I only possessed a five-pound note, which
my father had given me; this I lent, but never
saw it again. Consequently I can truly say
that I started life in Paris penniless. The next
morning I traced my way across Paris again to
Mr. Ostervald's house, and found him at home.
He had arranged that I should reside with a Swiss
family, but Newton Fielding, whom I subsequently
met, persuaded me to share his studio in Rue St.
Georges, as it was more convenient for my work.
I was chiefly occupied in water-colour painting,
and it is from this time that I date my first progress, learning all I could by watching Fielding
whilst he was at work. I also assisted him in
engraving. As we lived near to Montmartre we

frequently walked there to enjoy the extensive
view of the country towards St. Denis.

In the next year—1830—we left Rue St. Georges
and went to reside in Rue St. Honoré.   Here we
were engaged in making drawings on lithographic
stones, and I employed my leisure time in learning
the French language.   I soon acquired, by going
to the theatre as often as possible, the habit not
only of speaking fluently but also of thinking in
French, and later I translated one of Sir Walter
Scott's novels.

On the evening of the 26th July we were
suddenly startled by an uproar in Place Vendôme,
and on Fielding and myself rushing into the street
to ascertain the cause, we found an excited mob
crying out " À bas Charles X."   The mob proceeded down Rue St. Honoré, breaking all the
lamps which were hung by cords across the street,
and also many of those in front of the shops and
cafés at which the shutters had not been closed in
time.   The streets were quickly deserted by the
respectable part of the population, and the entire
city was in the hands of the Revolutionists.   On
the following day the Revolution commenced in
earnest ; barricades were erected in the streets by
the mob, and the soldiers fired upon the people.

I well remember on the 28th July, my eighteenth birthday, I was sent by Fielding to try and obtain some money which was owing by a picture-dealer living in Rue du Roule, but after climbing over several barricades I could proceed no further, and I was compelled to return after having run considerable risk for nothing. I should mention that both Newton Fielding and myself were obliged for safety to don tri-colour cockades, and I have still mine in my possession.

During this time our only food was bread, butter, and currants. One day we set out to the Marché des Innocents in order to try and obtain some provisions, and were about to cross a street to get to the river Seine, when we were suddenly stopped by a bystander, which act doubtless saved our lives, for in the next moment a volley was fired down the street by a detachment of soldiers, and the roadway was strewn with killed and wounded persons lying in all directions. On arriving at the Quai we had quickly to dip behind a wall in order to avoid more bullets which were flying about. It was most unpleasant, and I should never have ventured out had not Newton Fielding been so anxious for me to accompany him. We returned by the Quais to the Champs

Elysées, where we found a restaurant open. On entering we ascertained that we could have a "bifteck aux pommes," and were anticipating the pleasure of a good meal when the tramp of soldiers was heard arriving from Rambouillet. We were hurriedly turned out of the restaurant and the doors closed with "Allez-vous-en avec votre bifteck aux pommes." Hungry, tired, and disappointed, we wended our way back to our rooms and made a frugal repast with the last of our bread and currants.

Next morning (31st July) we again sallied forth in search of food, when we found everything changed. Charles X. had fled, the troops had been driven out, the populace had taken possession of the city, and there were rejoicings everywhere. The national guard was called out, and our tricolour cockades were more than ever required to ensure our safety. The weather was extremely hot, the streets were still barricaded, and not a vehicle was to be seen; and the mob, which had returned from pursuing the soldiers, were dressed in uniforms, helmets, etc., taken from the killed and wounded—a sight it was impossible ever to forget.

In the afternoon I went to the Palais Royal;

there on the balcony, with his family and officers, stood the Duc d'Orleans addressing the people below, and accepting the Lieutenant-Generalship of the Kingdom. Printed papers were thrown down amongst the crowd, and I managed to secure one of them, which I still retain as a memento of these exciting times. It reads as follows :—

HABITANS DE PARIS

Les Députés de la France, en ce moment réunis à Paris, m'ont exprimé le désir que je me rendisse dans cette capitale pour y exercer les fonctions de Lieutenant-Général du Royaume.

Je n'ai pas balancé à venir partager vos dangers, à me placer au milieu de votre héroïque population, et à faire tous mes efforts pour vous préserver des calamités de la guerre civile et de l'anarchie.

En rentrant dans la ville de Paris, je portais avec orgueil ces couleurs glorieuses que vous avez reprises, et que j'avais moi-même longtemps portées.

Les chambres vont se réunir ; elles aviseront aux moyens d'assurer le règne des lois, et le maintien des droits de la nation.

La Charte sera désormais une vérité.

LOUIS PHILIPPE D'ORLÉANS.

It was now plainly evident to Fielding and myself that, owing to the unsettled state of Paris, nothing could be done professionally for some time, and it was useless for us to remain there, so we decided to return to England.

On the 31st July, having hastily packed a few things which we could carry, we set off on foot, for, owing to the barricades, it was impossible to take a vehicle, to St. Denis, where we took the diligence to Rouen, and on our arrival there in the morning we were able to inform a detachment of the Garde Nationale, which was just leaving for Paris, that the Revolution was at an end.   In the afternoon we secured seats on an English coach which was leaving for Dieppe, and we thus passed a second night in travelling.   On arrival at Dieppe we were fortunate to find a steamer on the point of starting, and had just time to get on board.   After a rough crossing we found ourselves at midnight off Brighton, but the sea was so rough that it was impossible for us to land, although we were close enough to the chain-pier for the captain to impart, by aid of a speaking trumpet, to those on the pier the news that order was restored in Paris.   We eventually succeeded in landing at Shoreham, and took a cab back to Brighton, arriving at the Old Ship Hotel at one o'clock in the morning.   After an excellent supper I went to bed to enjoy a much-needed rest, and with an intense feeling of pleasure at being back in England after an absence of twelve months.   The next morning we took the coach to

NOTRE DAME, PARIS

(*Size* $9\frac{1}{8} \times 6\frac{3}{4}$ *inches*)

London, and my unexpected arrival was a great surprise to my family, who knew nothing of my movements, for in those days letters, costing a franc for postage, were few and far between.

Arrangements were at once made for me to again stay with Theodore Fielding at Croydon and to assist him in colouring prints. Whilst residing here I revisited Combe Hill and other haunts for the purpose of making sketches. After the expiration of six months I determined to rejoin Newton Fielding, who had returned to Paris, and on the 2nd February 1831 I again took the mail coach to Dover. On arrival there I found the sea so rough that the steamer was obliged to lie out in the bay, and the passengers had to be rowed to it in small boats, and, being at the mercy of the boatmen, each had to pay an exorbitant fee of five shillings. On reaching the steamer we were hauled on board by the sailors ; my shins were severely bruised, my Inverness cape flew over my head, and a packet of sandwiches, with which my mother had thoughtfully provided me, dropped into the sea.

On reaching Calais, after a crossing of ten hours, the tide was too low to allow the steamer to enter the harbour, so we were despatched in small boats to the sands, and from there we were taken

on women's backs to dry land. How well I
remember the woman who carried me saying,
"Tenez ferme," and bidding me clasp her tightly
round the neck. The journey by diligence to Paris
again took forty-eight hours, including the stoppages
en route for rest and refreshments. It was the last
occasion on which this part of the journey took me
so long, as in a year or two afterwards, with much
pressure, it was reduced to twenty-four hours. I
took up my old quarters with Newton Fielding in
Rue St. Honoré; later we lived in various other
parts of Paris, and finally settled in Rue Neuve St.
Georges. Shortly afterwards I became associated
with Thomas Shotter Boys, the clever but eccentric
artist, who had recently arrived from Brussels. In
later years I have seen it stated that Boys was
a pupil of Bonington, but if that had been the
case I certainly should have known of it. Boys
never spoke to me of having other than a mere
acquaintanceship with Bonington. Boys used
frequently to ramble about the ancient part of the
cité of Paris in search of old buildings to sketch.
I often accompanied him, and was encouraged by
him also to make sketches. In fact, I learnt a great
deal of the theory and practice of art from Boys,
and it was from him I first acquired my love for

making water-colour drawings of picturesque old churches and houses, for which subjects I have had a partiality ever since. I may mention that Paris was then as it had been for centuries. The streets, which were lighted by oil lanterns suspended down the middle by cords, were laid with cobble-stones with gutters running down the centre, and without any side pavements ; there was no sanitation, and whenever there was a storm the streets were flooded. The Tuileries were unfinished, and the whole of the Place de Carrousel was filled with houses, the stables of King Charles X., and book-stalls ; the churches, which had been damaged during the Revolution, were unrestored, and the Place de la Concorde and the Champs Elysées were almost a desert, whilst the Arc de Triomphe, commenced by Napoleon I., was still surrounded with scaffolding. In spite of all these detriments Paris, with its boulevards, was then more picturesque than it is at the present time. The immense alterations and improvements which were commenced by Louis Philippe, and carried on by Napoleon III., render it difficult for me now to recognise many of the old quarters which I knew then so well.

Baron Triqueti lived in the same house in which I

resided.   Once a week he used to invite his friends, including myself, to meet at his studio in the evenings, when we sketched armour or any other objects which he had previously arranged.   At a later period he became celebrated for designing and casting the bronze gates of the Madeleine; he was also commissioned by Queen Victoria to execute some decorative work in the Memorial Chapel at Windsor.   Triqueti married the youngest daughter of Mrs. Foster, a widow of a chaplain to the British Embassy, and Mr. Ambrose Poynter, father of the President of the Royal Academy, married the eldest daughter.   Mrs. Foster held weekly receptions at her house, to which I was frequently invited, and there I often met people from England.   I continued to make drawings for Newton Fielding, which he used to touch up and add a duck or some object, and eventually they became known as Callow-Fielding drawings.   We were very badly off at this period, as there was little or no sale for works of art; besides, Fielding was very unwell and unable to do much painting.   To show to what straits we were put, I will mention an incident which happened.   Fielding and I went to dine at a restaurant.   My dinner cost twenty-five sous, but Fielding could only muster up fifteen sous to lend me after paying for his own. As a last resource I took two or three drawings to a dealer and tried to sell them to him, but I was not successful; and I was returning to my lodgings, very depressed, when my eyes lighted upon a piece of silver lying on the ground in Place Vendôme, and it proved to be a ten-sous piece, just the sum required to make up the necessary amount for my dinner.

In the next year, 1832, thanks to Boys, I became more diligent in making sketches both in pencil and water colours, and many a happy day I spent in making short excursions to Versailles, St. Cloud, and Montmartre. I also made some large sketches from the bridges in Paris for Boys, for which he, knowing my fondness for reading, paid me in books.

In the early part of the year 1833 Newton Fielding married and returned to England. I went to reside with my Swiss friend Himley, an engraver, who provided me with copper plates to engrave; and it was at his instigation that I put my first savings of twenty francs into a Bank, which eventually proved to be a good beginning for me. I did not ·reside long with Himley, as in the month of May I left him and took an atelier with

T. S. Boys in Rue de Bouloy.   Whilst there I was
introduced to Samuel Prout, who called on one
occasion to see Boys.   My affairs now took a more
prosperous turn, and by working early and late
I was enabled to save sufficient money to take a
trip to England; even during this holiday I was
not idle, for I made a sketch of Pall Mall and
others at Richmond for Boys.

During my stay in London I called upon
George Cooke, the line engraver, who was living
at Barnes Terrace, to deliver a present from Boys.
He received me very kindly and asked me to stay
to dinner, when I met his son, E. W. Cooke, the
marine painter; he was then engaged upon his
etchings of London Bridge, and was just coming
into notice.   We exchanged some drawings, and his
father made me a present of several India-proof
impressions from his Turner plates, a valuable
gift which gave me great pleasure.   Boys had also
commissioned me to convey a present of a Turkish
sword to John Constable, the Royal Academician,
and I felt much gratified in meeting him.   It
proved to be the only time I saw Constable, as
he died before I came to England again.

On my return to Paris I accompanied a Mr.
Schweiter on a visit to a Mr. Vandermere, who lived

HASTINGS—FISHING BOATS, EARLY

(Size 18 × 11¾ inches)

at Royaumont, about ten leagues from Paris. We made part of the journey on foot in order to do some sketching. We were well received by the Vandermeres, and stayed with them some days, making numerous water-colour sketches of very interesting ruins of an old abbey, and also of the beautiful park with an ornamental piece of water. The adjoining mansion was inhabited by the Marquis de Bellisin, who invited us to make day excursions with him in the neighbourhood and to dinner in the evenings, with music and dancing afterwards. Altogether this was a most enjoyable visit.

In December of this year the boat containing the Luxor, having been towed from Egypt to Havre and up the Seine to Paris, was moored close to the Place de la Concorde, when the obelisk was hauled on a staging, erected for the purpose, to the pedestal on which it now stands. I made a sketch of the boat containing the obelisk on the spot.

In 1834 Boys gave up his atelier in Rue de Bouloy, and I took it on by myself, and remained there until I finally left Paris. About this time I had made quite a reputation for putting effects into other artists' works, chiefly on wood blocks

and drawings for engravings. Two important
instances I can remember; one was an extensive
publication on North America, carried out by a
German prince, assisted by Bodmer, a German
artist; the other was a grand work on Versailles,
containing a collection of engravings after the
paintings there. Having now a studio to myself,
I started a drawing class, and many of my pupils
were members of the old French nobility, including
the Comte de Faucigny, Viscomte de Rouget, his
cousin, Comte de Nicolai, and many others. I
recollect exchanging several of my drawings and
sketches with Comte de Faucigny for a beautiful
Louis XIV. clock, and others with a Madamoiselle
Naudet for old pistols, swords, and other curiosities
which helped to furnish my atelier.

In this year I exhibited at the Salon a large
water-colour drawing of "A View from Richmond,"
composed from a sketch done when I was last in
England. It attracted considerable attention, as
the art of water-colour painting was practically
unknown in Paris at the time. Shortly after
the opening of the exhibition, much to my
surprise, I received a visit to my studio, on the
sixième étage, from an equerry of King Louis
Philippe, to inquire whether I was willing to

teach drawing and painting to the King's son, the Duc de Nemours. Of course I readily consented, and felt very proud at having been selected for the honour. I gave the first lesson to the Prince at 8 A.M. on the 12th March 1834, at the Tuileries. On my first introduction to Royalty I was very nervous, especially as I spoke French imperfectly, but his Royal Highness quickly put me at my ease, and all my feelings of nervousness vanished. Shortly afterwards the Duc informed me that his sister, the Princesse Clémentine d'Orleans, commanded my presence, when I learned that she also wished to receive lessons in water-colour painting.

The room in which I gave lessons to the Duc was on the first floor, with windows looking on to the Tuileries gardens. Occasionally the governor of the Tuileries or some of the Duc's personal friends would come and chat on all kinds of subjects quite freely before me. The Princess took her lessons in a room on the ground floor, overlooking the Place de Carrousel. We used to sit at one of the windows, the lady-in-waiting, Madame Angeley, always being present. I gave lessons to the Princess twice a week nearly all the year round, but in summer at Neuilly or St. Cloud, and always at eight o'clock in the morning.

We sketched from a tent at Neuilly, and it was there I first had the honour of being introduced to the Queen; her Majesty came to see the progress made by the Princess, who was most constant in her attendance, and seldom missed a lesson during the seven years I taught her; in fact, until I left Paris. On leaving, after each lesson, I was given an order for twenty francs from Madame Angeley, and when these orders reached twenty, I presented them at the Bank, and received the money, viz. four hundred francs in five-franc pieces, which I carried away in a bag. I also gave some lessons to the Prince de Joinville. I cannot speak too highly in praise of this charming family; they were always amiable, kind, and studying to do whatever they thought would give me pleasure. These were amongst my happiest days in France.

My drawings now commanded a ready sale, and I had no difficulty in disposing of them to the dealers. I received forty francs for a drawing of a canal near Croydon, which was a good price for me at that time.

During this year John Lewis, the distinguished member of the Old Water-Colour Society, called at my atelier, on his way from Spain back to

RUE DE LA GROSSE HORLOGE, ROUEN

(*Size 25¼ x 18½ inches*)

England, to see T. S. Boys, who of course had left. "So you are a water-colour painter," he said on examining my works. He expressed himself so pleased with them that he advised me to send some to the Old Water-Colour Society with an application to become an Associate, but, not thinking that he was in earnest, I did not follow his advice at the moment. He remained for some time in Paris, in the Rue de Richelieu, working indefatigably on his Spanish paintings. On several occasions I posed for him as a model, once for my ear, and on another occasion wearing a cap of Zumalcarrequi, a Spanish chieftain.

During this period the French school of oil painting was very prolific in artists, such as Ingres, Horace Vernet, De la Roche, De la Croix, Descamps, Gudin, Isabey, and Scheffer, all producing fine works, which were shown at the Salon Exhibitions. I used to go to the private views, which were attended by all the fashionable people in Paris. Later, many of the painters just mentioned were engaged to carry out an idea of Louis Philippe to have pictures representing "toutes les gloires de la France" painted to fill the galleries at Versailles. Almost any painter could on application obtain a com-

mission for the work. On one occasion my friend
M. Schweiter was commissioned to paint the
portrait of a general; he had nothing to guide
him but the military dress of the period. In fact,
this was the case with most of the portraits which
were painted, as the King was imperious in having
his idea carried out as rapidly as possible.

In May 1835 I made my first walking tour,
and was accompanied by my old fellow-pupil,
John Edge, and a Jersey man named Larbarlestier,
who had come to Paris to assist in engraving for
a work which was being produced. We first took
the diligence to Rouen, thence we walked beside
the Seine to Jumiĕges, where there is a most
interesting ruin of an abbey, situated beside the
river. The next day we followed the right bank
of the Seine to Quillebœuf, but before reaching
there we had to cross in a ferry boat over the
river where it is very broad, and, being at low
tide, there was a great extent of mud-bank,
which prevented our boat approaching the land,
so the ferryman had to carry each of us ashore,
complaining at our weight, as well he might,
with our knapsacks included. We proceeded to
Honfleur, where we made some sketches, and on
the next day crossed over to Havre. Here

Larbarlestier left us, and Edge and myself took the steamer to Southampton. After touring on foot round the Isle of Wight we went to Portsmouth, and walked to Winchester, making a large number of sketches on the way, and finally took the coach to London. This tour proved to be a very pleasant one, and in this manner I was enabled to make sketches of many interesting places unfrequented by travellers. I afterwards went on a visit to some relatives at Lowestoft, my father's birthplace, and on returning to London I at once proceeded back to Paris with John Edge, taking with me my brother John, who was then a lad of thirteen years of age.

In this year I was offered an appointment as artist to a scientific expedition round the world, but being too much occupied in teaching and making a series of drawings on deep-sea fishing for my Swiss friend Himley, I declined the post.

My object in bringing my brother with me to Paris was to try and induce him to become an artist, although he had no ambition to take up art. He wished to be a sailor, but by degrees I persuaded him to go to the Louvre and copy the paintings there. After a time he took great interest in his work and made many excellent copies of the old

masters. I also used to study at the Louvre
whenever I could spare the time, and made
numerous copies of the paintings by Rubens,
Titian, Ostade, Salvator Rosa, and many others.
They are still in my possession.

IN THE HIGH STREET, SOUTHAMPTON

(Size 15½ × 18 inches.)

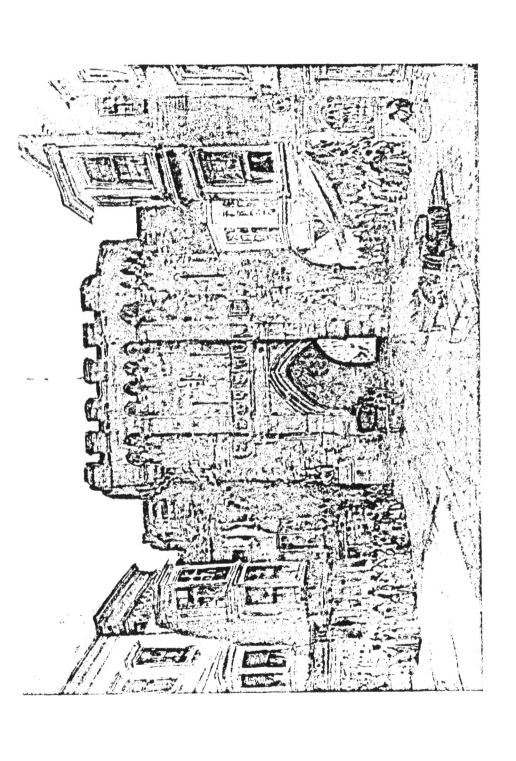

COURTRAI.

CHAPTER III

A WALKING TOUR THROUGH THE SOUTH OF FRANCE

IN the year 1836, after sending to an Exhibition at Cambrai a water-colour painting for which I was awarded a silver medal, I determined to make a walking tour through the south of France, leaving Jack Edge and my brother to carry on the work in my atelier.

The following account of this tour is extracted from a diary which I kept at the time:—

June 6.—We, *i.e.* myself, a German friend

31

named Soherr, and his dog, left Paris by diligence at eight o'clock in the evening for Chartres, and the weather being fine, we had a pleasant journey.

June 7.—A fine view of the town with the cathedral on a hill as we approached *Chartres* at six o'clock in the morning. A man on the diligence recommended us to some lodgings, which turned out to be a shoemaker's. We could not see the interior of the cathedral as the roof had unfortunately been burnt three days previously, so visited the churches of St. Pierre and St. André, where we found a great many curious monuments.

June 8.—At eleven o'clock we started off with our knapsacks and walked to *Bonneval,* a distance of seven leagues,[1] arriving there in the evening, very tired and weary, as we were not accustomed to long walks. After dinner we visited the fourteenth-century church; we were obliged to go there in our slippers as we were so footsore.

June 9.—After breakfast I made some sketches whilst Soherr, who was an architect, took some measurements of the church. We then started for *Châteaudun,* reaching that place at five o'clock. We visited the old château, surmounted by a fine tower of the sixteenth century.

[1] 1 league = 2 miles, 743 yards.

In the evening we started off again, and slept in an auberge on the roadside.

June 10.—After starting at half-past seven in the morning we reached a village, where we had breakfast, and, as the weather was so warm, we rested here till the evening, when we continued our walk to *Orleans,* where we arrived in the dark. We tried to put up at the Hôtel de la Boule d'Or, but because we were wearing blouses, on account of the dust, they refused to admit us, so we went to the Hôtel de France, where we fortunately ran across an English friend, named Talbot, who had previously arranged to meet us at Orleans and accompany us on the tour.

June 11. — Visited the cathedral, built by Henri IV., and made sketches of the river Loire, which, with its fine bridge and boats with large white sails, was very picturesque.

June 12.—Quitted Orleans at 7.30 A.M. and walked beside the Loire to the village of *Meung,* where we breakfasted; afterwards Talbot and I smoked and rested outside the auberge, whilst Soherr made some measurements of the church. I had placed a wine-glass on the ground, and an old woman accidentally broke it. The daughter of the house thereupon roundly abused her and made her cry, all because of a trifling damage of two sous, which I paid. Afterwards we visited the church, and found it to be nothing remarkable; but this was the way with Soherr all the time we were together; he made drawings of the worst and left the best. In the afternoon we continued beside the Loire to *Beaugency*. Passing through a village we saw a procession carrying the Host, it being a fĕte day; the villagers had hung up sheets against the walls for the want of tapestry. I did not expect to see so much religious devotion so near Paris. The pretty town of Beaugency was also *en fête*; we arrived too late to see the procession, but the sides of the houses were still covered with *toile* and the streets strewn with flowers. In the evening we went on the fine old bridge, with twenty-five arches over the river, and saw a beautiful sunset effect, but it was too dark to sketch it.

June 13.—Arose at 6 A.M. to make a sketch from the river; afterwards set off along a road beside the Loire, which is here very beautiful, to *St. Laurent*, where we breakfasted, and then we went on to the *Château de Chambord*, belonging to the Duc de Bordeaux.

June 14.—Got up early and visited the château,

CHÂTEAU D'AMBOISE.

From a Water-Colour Drawing made in 1836.

examining every part of it, even going on the roof for the sake of the view; the house contains a very curious double spiral staircase. After early breakfast we walked to *Blois* (four leagues), where we arrived about mid-day, and put up at the Hôtel de la Tĕte Noire. Visited the curious old château, which is now the barracks, also the churches of St. Nicholas and St. Louis, and afterwards made two sketches of the picturesque town from the river. On returning to our hotel we were accosted by a gendarme, who demanded our passports in a very insolent manner. I informed him that if he would come to the hotel we would produce them. He then became very abusive, and said that foreigners ought to have their passports always with them. Eventually he followed us to the hotel, where we met the *maître* on the doorstep, who had a lively discussion with the gendarme for about half an hour. Eventually he was sent about his business, and we all went to the head office to lodge a complaint. In the evening we had two bottles of wine, and invited the *maître d'hôtel* to join us, as he had so kindly taken our part.

June 15.—Sorry to have to leave at 7 A.M., as we were much pleased with Blois. Passed through *Chailles, Monthou,* and *Sambin,* breakfasting at the

last-named village, the country now becoming
more fertile and rich, and arrived, by a beautiful
road, at *Montrichard*, on the river Cher. A steep
ascent leads up to the village, with houses built on
rocks on either side of the road, and the ruins of a
fine old castle at the summit. We spent a quiet
evening on the banks of the river, a lovely
spot.

June 16.—I was up at 5 A.M., and made four
sketches before breakfast. Afterwards we walked
to *Chénonceaux*, where, leaving our knapsacks at an
auberge, we went to see the château, which still
contains the fine old furniture of François I. and
Henri II, who lived here, including the beds of
Diane de Poitiers and of Catherine de Medicis.
We then set off to *Amboise*, arriving there in time
for dinner. In the evening we visited the château,
belonging to Louis Philippe; the house, being late
Gothic, is not remarkable for its architecture, but
there is a very pretty garden.

June 17.—Arose again at 5 A.M., and made
a few sketches, but was very disappointed with
Amboise. We set off for Tours, and ten minutes
after we had started it began to rain hard. As it
seemed to be set in for a wet day, we plodded on
through it for four leagues, and became soaked

TOURS.

From a Water-Colour Drawing made in 1836.

to the skin. Fortunately the sun came out and dried us by the time we reached *Vouvray*, where we stopped to have some refreshments. On reaching *Tours* we went to the Hôtel de France. I was not impressed with the town, and the cathedral has nothing very remarkable, excepting some fine stained-glass windows.

June 18.—Did a little sketching, but could find nothing very interesting. We were detained at Tours for our washing till seven in the evening. Blew up the washerwoman and left for *Luynes*, where did not arrive until it was quite dark.

June 19.—Up at 5 A.M., and ready to start, but Soherr kept us waiting until eight o'clock whilst he was writing a letter. This was the first little rift in the lute, which ultimately caused our parting company. We eventually set off for *Langeais*, and met a large number of country people going to market at Luynes ; the men all wore large black hats and many of the girls were very pretty. After passing Langeais on the way to Bourgueil, Soherr said he would take another road because we would not agree to go with him to Angers ; so we went to an auberge to settle the matter over a bottle of wine, and we persuaded him that it was just as near to go to Bourgueil and then to turn off to Angers.

We were caught in several showers before reaching *Bourgueil,* where we stayed the night.

June 20.—Bid good-bye at 6 A.M. to Soherr, who turned off to go to Candes, whilst Talbot and I kept on the direct road to *Saumur,* where we arrived very hungry. There is nothing like a five leagues' walk to give one an appetite for breakfast. Went to the castle and had a fine view of the Loire and the country around ; later to the Druidical remains ; nothing remarkable except for the size of the stones. In the evening Soherr arrived at our hotel.

June 21.—On the previous evening we had half promised the *maître d'hôtel* to go with him to Candes, and we were called at half-past three in the morning, but made various excuses and let him go alone. After again bidding good-bye to Soherr, who started off to Angers, Talbot and I set off along a pretty road to *Candes,* meeting our *maître* on his way back. The church at Candes is very beautiful. We continued on our journey to *Fontevrault,* where there is a large prison capable of holding fifteen hundred prisoners and an old church of the 12th century. We obtained permission to see the interior of the latter, in which are the tombs of Henry II. and Richard Cœur-de-Lion of England, with recumbent figures in sandstone. After resting we proceeded to *Loudun*, a curious old town which had formerly been fortified; a Roman tower, one of seven, still exists. The town stands on a height in the centre of a large plain with no village near it. It can be seen for a great distance, and when we were at Fontevrault, five leagues away, the town appeared to be quite close.

June 22.—Left next morning for Mirebeau, and on passing through a small village we heard several voices from an auberge calling upon us to stop. We discovered that these were three young conscripts going to join their regiments at Poitiers and that they wished to accompany us on the road; they were surrounded by about twenty of their friends, and there was a good deal of drinking going on. We were obliged to *trinquer* some very bad wine with them all, including a dragoon *en congé*, who said to the conscripts "souvenez-vous que vous êtes toujours français." Eventually, after a great deal of leave-taking, the three conscripts set off with us. We walked two leagues, thinking all the way how we could get rid of our friends when we reached an auberge. Having treated them to some wine, we told them we were going to remain for some time, at which they seemed very sorry and insisted on our having some *petits verres* with them; they then left, but one, the best of the lot, stayed behind for a few seconds and asked permission to embrace us, *il était si triste!* so we could not refuse... Later two carters offered us a lift, which we gladly accepted, though the seats were not very soft, as the cart was laden with casks. We passed by *Mirebeau*, not entering into the town, which is surrounded with walls and towers, and went twol cagues farther to *Etaples*, where we put up at an inn. After having some dinner we took a walk in the neighbourhood, and, on returning to the inn, we were greatly surprised to find that our three conscripts had just arrived with numerous others, all very hot and tired out. They suggested that, as we were all going in the same direction the next morning, we should start together for Poitiers. When we retired to rest we were greatly annoyed to find a room with five beds, four of which were filled with conscripts, the remaining one being left for us. As there was no help for it, we made ourselves as comfortable as we could.

June 23.—The next morning we were awakened by the conscripts dressing, but we lay quite quiet until they had all gone downstairs, deciding to remain in bed until they had started, and it was with great pleasure we heard them tramp off. Later we set out for Poitiers, and while passing through the village of *Migné* we saw women riding astride on horseback, cleverly tucking in their petticoats. After walking four and a half leagues we reached *Poitiers*, well known for its battlefield. It is an interesting town, containing many curiosities, including the remains of a Roman amphitheatre. Visited the very fine cathedral of St. Pierre and the church of St. Jean. As it was the *veille* of the latter saint, bonfires were lit by the priests in the town. Had a beautiful view from the height which is on one side of the town.

June 24.—Made some sketches in the morning, and left Poitiers in the afternoon, and, passing through the village of *Croutille*, with a very pretty country all the way, arrived at *Vivonne* at nine o'clock.

June 25.—Up at 6 A.M., a splendid morning, so set out from Vivonne at once. The weather became so very hot that we stayed at a village café until late in the afternoon, and then proceeded to *Chaunay*, where we dined. It was such a lovely night that we decided not to go to bed, but to continue our walk throughout the night. At the village of *Ruffec* we were asked by a gendarme for our passports. He

6

was a veritable *grogneur*. Nevertheless we went to his cabin and had some wine with him. After bidding him adieu we continued on our road, getting sleepy and very cold near sunrise ; about a hundred conscripts passed us. At last we reached *Mansle* at five o'clock in the morning, very tired indeed, having walked seven leagues during the day and ten at night. We went to a café to have some hot coffee and milk, and whilst it was being prepared we both fell asleep.

June 26.—Woke up after an hour and had our coffee, then set off for Angoulême, seven leagues farther. As we became very footsore, we stopped at a village from 9 A.M. till 3.30 P.M. Eventually, after mounting a steep hill, we arrived at *Angoulême* and put up at the Hôtel Périgueux. After dinner we turned into bed. What enjoyment! What happiness !

June 27.—Got up for breakfast, but slept nearly the whole of the day. In the evening we went on the ramparts, which surround the town ; saw a lovely sunset and the full moon rise. In the interesting old town are some towers remaining of an old castle, and the ancient cathedral has some curious sculptures on the exterior. The country around is rich but flat, and the river Charente winds prettily through the plain. Here we first saw oxen used in place of horses for drawing carts.

June 28.—The weather piping hot. A regiment arrived. I never saw soldiers so covered with dust. Made some sketches in the broiling sun. At lunch we met an old military officer who had been through the Russian campaign; he tried to make us believe that he knew everything, and told us that in Holland cows were fastened up with silver chains. There was also a young man who talked very grandly about the number of crimes he would commit for the sake of his country. We had just heard of an attempt which had been made on the King's life. Took the coach to Barbezieux, passing on the way the ruin of an old abbey at the village of *La Couronne*, and at *Roullet* an old church of the same period as the cathedral at Angoulĕme. On arrival at *Barbezieux* we were followed by the Sous-Préfet, who inquired whether we were Poles, but on learning that we were English he became very polite and apologised for following us. At the inn the host's daughter, who was very beautiful, sang charmingly. We were much taken with her, and made two clerks very jealous because we got into conversation with her.

June 29.—Up at 5.30 A.M. to catch the coach at six, and owing to the stupidity of the maid we had nothing to eat except a piece of bread until the coach stopped at *Montlieu* for *déjeûner*. There were ten passengers in the coach, and it being very hot weather, we were nearly stifled. After passing through a beautiful country we reached *St. André*. We walked forward to the banks of the Gironde and saw the ruins of a castle. The river here is very broad, and there being no bridge, we crossed by a ferry, the boat being drawn by a rope attached to a drum, like a mill, turned by horses. We were all packed in the boat, including the coach and horses, and arrived safely on the other side of the river, although there was some alarm amongst the lady passengers owing to the horses getting fidgety. We started on the coach again. Driving through the vine country for two hours, we came to the hills close to Bordeaux on which the best vines are cultivated, then crossed the bridge over the Garonne into *Bordeaux*, where Talbot and myself stayed at Hôtel de Rouen.

June 30.—Spent an intensely hot day seeing the sights of the town, and attended the launch of a vessel at high tide. Could not sleep at night on account of the heat.

July 1.—Got up at 6 A.M. and made some sketches in the early morning; as the weather was still extremely hot, could do very little during the day.

July 2.—Walked out to St. André and saw the church of St. Michel. On our return we met Soherr, who had just arrived, and we talked over our respective adventures.

July 3.—Visited the church of St. Severin. I determined to continue my tour in the night on account of the heat. Talbot tried to persuade me to wait another day for him, but as he would go only as far as Agen I adhered to my determination. At 11.30 P.M. Talbot and Soherr accompanied me to the gate of the town, and I started off alone for Langon. Being a lovely and warm night, I rested by the roadside. I never felt so lonely in my life; thought of all those at home. Walked nine leagues and stopped at a village near *Castres*.

July 4.—Slept nearly all day, and set out for *Langon* in the evening. Put up at an inn where every one spoke a patois which I could not understand. Went down to the river and saw steamers arrive from Bordeaux.

July 5.—Up at 4 A.M. and crossed the bridge just as the sun was rising, a charming effect with

Langon on one side of the river and a ruin of an old castle on the other; passed several villages in a very pretty country and reached *La Réole*, where I took the steamer to *Marmande*.

July 6.—Weather became less oppressive, and I determined to profit by it, making an early start, and at 10 A.M. reached *Tonneins*, famous for manufacturing tobacco. Was told that on a clear day the Pyrenees could be seen from here. Pressed on, passed the town of *Aiguillon*, and arrived at *Port St. Marie*, where I stayed the night at an inn in a room overlooking the river, which is broad and fine.

July 7.—Started at 4.30 A.M. along a pretty road, with tobacco plantations and a quantity of corn, which was being reaped, on either side; the hills were now becoming more lofty. Overtook a regiment on the way to Toulouse; the officers were walking with the men, and all were covered with dust. Passed *St. Hilaire* and arrived at *Agen* at 8 P.M., putting up at the Hôtel de France. Made some sketches, but nearly the whole of the town is hidden by large trees along a fine promenade beside the river. I had followed the Garonne nearly all the way from Bordeaux.

July 8.—Up late. Visited the very old church

of St. Caprais and the picturesque Hôtel de Ville, which dates from 1665. In the evening took a walk by the river, and saw hundreds of women bathing—quite a usual custom.

July 9.—Took the coach to Auch, and as the road is very hilly and the weather still hot, I am glad of the ride. Had *déjeûner* at *Lectoure*, a town which has been the birthplace of many generals of the French Army, including Montebello, a maréchal under Napoleon. *Auch* is prettily situated on a hill, and the cathedral, being built in a prominent position, is seen from a great distance. Went to see the famous stained-glass windows which it contains. As a coach for Tarbes arrived from Toulouse, I decided to continue my journey by it.

July 10.—Arrived at *Tarbes* at 7 A.M. I had slept on the coach as far as *Rabastens*. Soon after leaving this place I first saw the Pyrenees, which I had long wished to do; the view made a lasting impression on my mind. A long line of mountains rose from an expansive plain and extended as far as the eye could reach. Above a delicate distant blue, partly hid by mist, could be seen small quantities of snow. The mountains had a grand appearance, and I longed to be amongst them. On reaching the Hôtel du Grand Soleil at Tarbes

I immediately set off to get a nearer view of the mountains. On my return to the town I once more put my knapsack on my back and left with a light heart for Lourdes. How I enjoyed myself with the beautiful view in front of me! What a splendid sight! What a variety of colours and forms! I wished for some one to be with me to partake of my pleasure. I made some sketches, but the scene changed every instant. How happy I felt at seeing mountains for the first time! They were so beautiful. I never felt so happy. I sang for joy. On entering a pass I came to a village, which on inquiry I understood to be Lourdes. Being Sunday, all the inhabitants were strolling about the street. I asked for the hotel, but as they only spoke a patois, they did not understand me, but pointed to a place which I discovered to be a low, dirty inn with a lot of men drinking. I was shown by a woman into a room with two beds, and when I expostulated she tried to console me by saying it was only the servant's bed. I ordered some supper, and whilst waiting outside the door of the inn for it to be prepared, all the men who had been drinking jumped out of a window and stood talking and eyeing me in a peculiar manner. Later two drunken men entered;

they were going to Lourdes, which I now found out to be a league farther; they were very curious to know all about me, and obliged me to drink with them. When they discovered that I was also on the way to Lourdes, they wanted me to accompany them. On my refusing, they whispered to me on the sly that the place was not to be trusted, and told me about a murder and the body being thrown in a pit. I began to be really frightened, and when supper was at last served it was so bad that I could not touch it. Fortunately a cart was driven up to the door of the inn, and the carter invited me to ride with him to Lourdes, which I instantly decided to do. The woman of the house looked very black when she saw that I was determined to leave, and I put my large knife up my sleeve as a precaution, but the carter soon dissolved my fears. He turned out to be a good fellow, and we had a long talk over his campaign in Spain. We reached *Lourdes* all safely at ten o'clock at night; the carter directed me to a decent hotel, and after bidding him adieu I entered and ordered a good supper.

July 11.—Up and off by 6 A.M. Am now in the interior of the Pyrenees, surrounded on all sides by beautiful mountains in the greatest variety, with a torrent, the Gave, rushing through the valley of Argeles, in the middle of which are the ruins of several castles. Arrived at *Argeles*, where I breakfasted, then walked two more leagues to *Pierrefitte*. After having rested there during the heat of the day, I climbed a very steep road by the side of a mountain, with an impetuous torrent on the other side, leaping from rock to rock and falling in deep cascades; the valley was nearly closed in with mountains, so grand and sublime. It was one of the finest walks I ever had in my life to *Cauterets*, where I took up my quarters.

July 12.—Started off on an expedition to *Lac de Gaube* without my knapsack. Met several invalids being carried from the Baths higher up the mountains, and continued to ascend a good road, passing a very pretty cascade, to *Pont d'Espagne*, which I crossed, and entered into the valley beyond, the wildest I had yet seen ; of quite a different character of scenery with huge masses of rocks partly covered with pines. Afterwards I climbed up a path to the lake, beautifully situated, being entirely surrounded by mountains of great height, towering above it. Here I met three Englishmen, with whom I returned to Cauterets.

On the way we met some Spanish smugglers— queer-looking fellows.

July 13.—Left Cauterets with great regret at six o'clock in the morning and retraced my steps to Pierrefitte, intending to go to Barĕges; but I changed my mind and continued back through Argeles to Lourdes, where I turned off to the right to *Bagnères-de-Bigorre.* I arrived in the evening, having walked fourteen leagues, but I was not much tired, as so many beautiful views did not give me time to think of fatigue.

July 14.—Remained at Bagnĕres-de-Bigorre all day, but was disappointed with the place.

July 15.—Up at 5 A.M., and started for St. Gaudens along a charming road; passed through *Escaliadieu* and *Lannemezan,* having breakfast at the latter village. Arrived at *St. Gaudens* very tired, having walked all day. Took my departure at ten o'clock the same night in a coach for *Toulouse,* where I arrived at eight o'clock the next morning, having slept during nearly the whole of the journey.

July 16.—Remained all day at Toulouse and visited the quays and bridges; tried to make some sketches, but a storm forced me to seek shelter.

July 17.—After walking on the promenade of

Lafayette, etc., and seeing the churches of St. Étienne and St. Sernin, I made various sketches. I took the coach to Narbonne in the evening.

July 18.—Travelled all night and the greater part of the next day on the coach. There was little to see on the road excepting the picturesque town of *Carcassonne,* with its old tower situated on a hill and surrounded by walls. As usual, I was more fatigued by riding than walking, besides being almost stifled by heat and dust. Arrived at *Narbonne* at last. The town is famous for honey. It is situated on a plain, and has an antiquated appearance. A branch of the Canal du Midi passes through the town, but I was unable to make a sketch of it, as it is so closed in by walls.

July 19.—Up at 5.30 A.M. and set off to Béziers, and soon caught a distant view of the Mediterranean. Stopped at *Béziers* to lunch and rested during the heat of the day ; continued my walk to Pézenas ; began to feel very tired, as one of my feet was very painful. Fortunately a man riding a donkey overtook me, and put my knapsack in his basket, which was a great relief. We chatted all the way to *Pézenas.* I went to Hôtel des Trois Pigeons, and soon to bed, as I was never before so tired.

July 20.—Woke at 5 A.M., and started along a pretty road bordered with lime, almond, and olive trees; stopped at a spring and rested my foot, which still troubled me, and reached *Mèze* in time for breakfast, a pretty place on the Étang du Thau. The boats with lateen sails give it quite an Italian appearance. I decided to rest here for a day.

July 21.—Took the coach to *Montpellier*, arriving at 2 P.M. Visited the cathedral and the promenade, where there was an exceedingly fine view, the mountains on one side and the sea on the other. Met a Monsieur Fils at the hotel, and we arranged to go together to Toulon.

July 22.—Up at 5.30 A.M. and made some sketches with Monsieur Fils, who left by coach for Nimes, where I joined him later.

July 23.—Arrived at *Nîmes* at 4 A.M., having travelled by coach all night. Visited the Amphi-theatre and the Maison Carrée; afterwards went to the Gardens to see the Temple of Diana and the Bath of Augustus. Took the coach with Monsieur Fils to *Beaucaire*, with its old castle, prettily situated on the Rhone, with Tarascon on the other side of the river. Had arranged to take the boat in the evening to Arles, but it never

arrived, and as the town was so full on account of
a fair being held, we were compelled to find some
lodgings a little way out of it; even then we could
only get a mattress on a floor.

July 24.—We were so disturbed by flies that
we were glad to get out of our lodgings at four
o'clock in the morning, when we met a man, whose
acquaintance we had made on the road to Beaucaire,
wandering about in search of his lodgings; on his
arrival he had taken some rooms, where he left his
luggage and put the key in his pocket, but he
forgot to note the name of the street or the
number of the house. After helping him for some
time without success we left him to his fate.
Took the steamer, which had arrived in the early
morning, to *Arles*, where we transferred into
another steamer for Marseilles. I was delighted
with the change from dusty roads. I climbed the
foremast and sat on the yard-arm till the steamer
reached the mouth of the river. At last I was on
the blue Mediterranean. The steamer took a turn
out to sea, and in a few hours we arrived at
Marseilles, which looks very fine on approaching it
from the bay, with the mountains behind it.

July 25.—Strolled about the town and visited
the harbour and fortifications. In the evening

took the coach for Toulon, along a road which passes through a very mountainous country.

July 26.—Arrived at *Toulon* at 4 A.M. and put up at the Hôtel de France. Fils having obtained a pass, we visited the Arsenal; the sight of so many criminals was revolting. I never saw such a set of wretches with every crime written on their faces; they were all dressed in red jackets and numbered, and nearly every one had chains on his legs. I was glad to get away.

July 27. — Up early and sketched all day. Saw a man-of-war come into the port, and climbed on the heights to obtain a view of the Iles d'Hyères. Returned in a coach to Marseilles. During the night, whilst walking up one of the hills, I saw the full moon through the mountains shining on the Mediterranean—a glorious sight.

July 28. — My twenty-fourth birthday. On arrival at Marseilles went to bed till 8 A.M. Visited the quays and made a number of sketches of merchantmen coming into harbour.

July 29.—Fils woke me at 2 A.M. to say good-bye, as he was starting for Sisteron. I was to leave by coach at six for Aix, but fell asleep again, and did not wake until a few minutes before that hour. Hurried into my clothes, but found the coach had already started, so got a man to carry my knapsack and ran after it, catching it up about a mile out of the town as it was ascending a hill ; arrived at *Aix* at 9 A.M. Intended to make some sketches, but unable on account of the heat. I had decided to take the coach to Avignon, but it was so full that I went by another one to Orgon.

July 30.—Arrived at *Orgon* at 3 A.M. Was told the coach for Avignon would pass through at 6 A.M., but they could not ensure my obtaining a seat, so I decided to walk. Had not proceeded far when the coach overtook me, and I was tempted by an offer to take me to *Avignon* for thirty sous. The picturesque town is entirely surrounded by walls, and has a pretty promenade with lime-trees on the banks of the Rhone, which is very broad here, and over it is a wooden bridge, and there are also remains of one built in the 12th century. Saw the Palace of the Popes, which has more the appearance of a prison with its severe towers ; also visited the cathedral, containing some fine monuments.

July 31.—Tried to sketch, but the wind blew so hard that it was impossible to do anything. Took the coach in the evening to *Orange.* Having the box seat and no overcoat, I was nearly frozen by the cold wind. Put up at a miserable inn. There was no bolt to my bedroom door, so I placed a chair against it and my money under my pillow. I was just dropping off to sleep when I heard a noise. I jumped out of bed and saw a man with a lantern. He made an excuse of wanting to fetch something, but I am not sure that he had not some other intention.

August 1.—Roamed about the town, and saw a very beautiful Roman triumphal arch. Determined if possible to continue my walk by side of the river—my original intention. I started across the country by a cross-road, but after some time I found myself on the main road only about three miles off Orange. I continued to *Mornas,* where I made a sketch of the picturesque castle of Montdragon, situated on a perpendicular rock above the village; then proceeded to *La Palude,* where I stopped the night at the Hôtel des Postes.

August 2.—Had experienced so much heat on the previous day that I got up early and was on the road again by 4 A.M.; rested at *Donzère.* After leaving this village I was overtaken by a *patache,* the worst description of coach ever invented, and I was, to my sorrow, tempted by an offer to take me to *Montélimar* for ten sous. I was almost suffocated by heat, and every bone in my body was

nearly dislocated by the jolting. Arrived at the
Hôtel des Princes at 10 A.M.; took a stroll by the
side of the little river which flows into the Rhone,
with a charming view of the Dauphině mountains
in the distance.

August 3.—Up again at 4 A.M. and started for
Valence, resting at *Loriol* on the road, which is
very beautiful as it approaches the Rhone. My
foot began to trouble me again, so I took a
seat on a coach, and arrived at *Valence* in the
afternoon.

August 4.—Decided to rest here all day and
made some sketches by the river.

August 5.—Started at 4 A.M. for Tain. Just
before reaching it the road passes close to the river,
and there is a beautiful view with Tain on one side
and Tournon, with the ruins of an old castle, on the
other. On account of the beauty of the place I
had intended to remain at *Tain*, but I got into
such bad quarters that I was quite disgusted.
Determined to walk on to St. Vallier. The weather
now seemed inclined to change, and some heavy
black clouds came up and produced some beautiful effects over the hills, but there was no rain.
How I longed for a shower! It was now about two
months since I had felt a drop of rain, and had

hardly seen a cloud; nothing but continuous blue sky and burning heat. Arrived at *St. Vallier*, and put up at a hotel which was worse than the one I had left, and as there was no other, I was compelled to stay. Rain came during the night, and everybody, including myself, was delighted. Everything was parched up, the grapes were very small, and there were neither vegetables nor grain.

August 6.—Took a seat in a small coach to *Lé Péage*, and from there I walked six leagues to *Vienne*, along a very interesting road close to the river, with a view of the hills opposite and the Dauphiné mountains in the distance. Visited the fine Gothic cathedral. Was much annoyed by being woke up in the middle of the night to admit a traveller to sleep in a spare bed which was in the room.

August 7.—Passed the day making sketches beside the river of the picturesque town.

August 8.—The last day of my tramp. Started at 4 A.M. as usual and walked to *Lyons*. Here I remained for some days waiting for remittances, which arrived on the 13th. I at once booked a seat in the banquette of the diligence for Paris, and started at ten o'clock the same evening. When we had passed Mâcon and Châlons we experienced a tremendous thunderstorm, the lightning being exceptionally vivid, which frightened the horses so much that the conductor had to get down and lead them. After having spent three days and nights on the road, passing through Auxerre and Sens, I arrived safely in Paris on Tuesday, the 16th August. During the nearly two months and a half which I had been absent, I had traversed 681 leagues, or about 1700 miles, and the entire cost of the journey was only twenty pounds.

TRENT.

CHAPTER IV

LIFE IN PARIS (*continued*)

ON the return from my tour I at once commenced hard work again with my pupils, and by
putting effects into numerous drawings on wood
by other artists, for Giradon and other publishers.
It was from Giradon that I obtained a copy of
Turner's "Southern Coast," and of "England and
Wales," the possession of which has always been a
great pleasure to me. I was always studying them
in those days, and I am sure they were a great
help to me in every way.

61

In the autumn of 1836 my old friend, Charles Bentley, came over to Paris on a visit. I was delighted to see him, and this was the first time Bentley, Edge, and myself had met together since we were pupils under Fielding.

In October, Bentley, Outhwaite (an engraver) and myself took a trip to Rouen and Havre, making sketches by the way. Outhwaite and I, after seeing Bentley off by steamer back to England, returned to Paris.

In the next year, 1837, I was fully engaged in making drawings for the work on North America, also in retouching the set of wood engravings for the *Gallery at Versailles*. Giradon introduced me to Charles Heath, the London publisher, who commissioned me to make a series of original drawings for a work to be entitled, *Les Fastes de Versailles*. Editions were subsequently published in Paris in French, and in London in English. For this purpose I obtained permission to visit the private gardens and the Trianon at Versailles. About this time the Comte de Noë called upon me to obtain some drawings for the Société des Amis des Arts, of which he was President. I supplied him with two paintings, one of which, "The Port of Marseilles," was won by King Louis

WIMBLEDON

(Size 10¼ × 7¼ inches)

Philippe in a lottery. I continued my acquaintance with the Count, and from time to time sold other drawings to him for lotteries. I was very busy with my pupils, and received commissions for water-colour paintings from picture-dealers both in Paris and London, so that I was enabled to add to my small savings which I had started at the Bank in 1834. Being sadly in need of a rest, I, accompanied by my brother John, paid a visit to England, first to London, and afterwards to Great Yarmouth, where I sketched boats and shipping scenes. Later I went with Bentley for a trip round the Isle of Wight, travelling to Portsmouth by coach. We both made numerous studies of marine subjects. On returning to Paris in November, I and my brother went by boat from London to Boulogne. On account of the tide the steamer was compelled to anchor off Dover all night, and crossed the Channel the next morning.

I sent a water-colour drawing to a local Exhibition at Boulogne-sur-Mer, for which I was awarded a silver medal. I was principally painting sea-pieces at the time; they were quite a novelty in Paris, and I received many orders for them from Durand-Ruel.

In the following year, 1838, the Princess

Clémentine requested to see the sketches which I had made in the South of France, and gave me a commission to make paintings from two of them. I was one day surprised, at my atelier, by a visit from Alexandre Dumas, the famous novelist, who came to invite me to join him in a trip to the South of France; he was going to write his *Impressions de Voyage*, and he wished me to supply the illustrations, but owing to my numerous pupils and many engagements I was compelled to decline his request.

Acting upon the advice of John Lewis and my friend Bentley, I sent three drawings to the Old Water-Colour Society in support of my candidature for election, and on the 15th February I received the gratifying intelligence that I had been unanimously elected an Associate. For some time previously it had been my ambition to become associated with this grand Society, yet when the news of my election reached me I could scarcely believe it to be true, not having sufficient confidence in my own powers to think that I should ever succeed. A new incentive for work in the future! The following notice appeared in the *Spectator* :—

The Water-Colour Society last week filled one of two vacancies by electing a Mr. William Callow, landscape and

FISHING BOATS OFF THE COAST O

(Size 10¾ × 7½ inches.)

marine painter, not known in this country, but who has studied in the French School, we have heard, and is of the dashing style of execution. There were several candidates, most of whom possessed as much merit as many of the present members, but the Society has wisely raised the standard of qualification, so that the future aspirants will be required to exhibit matured excellence to render them eligible.

I learnt later that Cattermole had strongly supported my candidature, and Copley Fielding, who had known me since I was quite a small boy, had spoken of me in the highest terms of praise. It was a rule of the Society not to elect, as an associate or member, an artist residing out of England, but an exception was made in my case, and being unable to leave Paris on account of my work, I sent my contributions to the first two Exhibitions from there. I became acquainted with the Comte Stackelberg, a Russian noble, and members of his family, also Baronne Mayendorff, and the family of Cherniticheff, Viceroy of Poland, many of whom became my pupils. John Lewis again stayed in Paris during this summer, and we frequently met at Schweiter's studio.

I returned to England to witness the Coronation of Queen Victoria, which I did both at Westminster and in the Park in company with Bentley. Whilst in London I called on Charles Heath, the

9

publisher, who gave me an introduction to J. M. W. Turner. On presenting myself at his residence in Queen Anne Street, the door was opened by his old housekeeper, who requested me to wait in the hall whilst she delivered the letter to Mr. Turner. To my surprise, Turner himself came out to me, and upon my asking permission to see his gallery, he abruptly though kindly said, "Go up." So upstairs I went, delighted not only at getting an opportunity of seeing his wonderful paintings, but at meeting the painter himself. It was a painful surprise, however, to find Turner's gallery in a most dilapidated condition. Many of the pictures, some on the ground and others leaning against the wall, were cracked and damaged ; the walls were in a deplorable state of damp, with the paper hanging down in strips. I remained a long time admiring his beautiful painting, and on going downstairs no one appeared, so I had quietly to let myself out at the front door without having an opportunity of thanking Turner for his kindness. My recollection of Turner is that of a short, dark man, inclined to stoutness, with a merry twinkle in his eye. The next time I met Turner was at Venice, at the Hotel Europa, where we sat opposite at meals and entered into conversation. One evening whilst I was enjoying a cigar in a gondola I saw Turner in another one sketching San Giorgio, brilliantly lit up by the setting sun. I felt quite ashamed of myself idling away my time whilst he was hard at work so late.

In the autumn of 1838 I made my first tour in Switzerland. I took the dilgence to Dijon, on which I made the acquaintance of a Mr. Forman, and we agreed to travel together. From Dijon we crossed the plains of Burgundy to Besançon and Pontarlier. From the latter place we took the Swiss post over the Jura mountains to Lausanne. Here, shouldering our knapsacks we started off and walked to Vevey, where, after making some sketches, we continued to Villeneuve, on the borders of the Lake of Geneva, and took the steamer to Geneva. We left the next day at 3 A.M., and walked along a beautiful road to Bonneville. Arrived very tired and knocked up by the heat. On the following day, after resting during the heat at Cluses, we reached St. Martin late in the evening. We then proceeded through the valley of Servoz and a beautiful gorge to the valley of Chamouny, surrounded by Mont Blanc and other mountains. We made an excursion to the Mer de Glace, taking a mule, which we rode in turns up to Montanvert, then across the ice up to Le Couvercle, and arrived at the Jardin, where we rested and returned to Chamouny. The next day we went with guides up Mont Blanc. We afterwards proceeded to Nantborrant; from there we went down to Les Chapieux, and ascended Col de la Seigne, where I made some sketches of the beautiful view, the Aiguilles and Mont Blanc above us, and Lake Combal and the Allée Blanche below. We then proceeded to Aosta. Next day we left with a party of eight and two guides for St. Rĕmy, the Hospital of St. Bernard, where we saw the monks, the famous dogs, and the chapel. I thought of Rogers' lines " promising bread to the hungry, and to the weary rest." From St. Rĕmy we descended to Liddes in a thunderstorm, and reached Martigny the same evening. On the following day I and Forman had to part company. I set out to Sion, and then proceeded up to Louèche, where I went with a guide up the rocks. Afterwards I walked to Thun, and took the steamer to Unterseen, beautifully situated on the lake, and proceeded to Interlaken. On the following day I hired a guide and went through the valley of Lauterbrunnen, visited the Staubbach, where the Jungfrau, covered with snow, could be seen, and climbed up the Wengern Alp, arriving at the châlet, where I was the only traveller. The next morning I was called by the innkeeper to see an avalanche. Afterwards I left for the valley of Grindelwald, crossing the Scheidegg at the foot of the Wetterhorn, and stopped at Rosenlaui, a very pretty spot. Saw during the descent the cascade of Reichenbach. Then proceeded to Meiringen, where I hired another guide and started for the Grimsel, turning on one side to see the beautiful waterfall of Handegg, and passing over immense blocks of granite to Grimsel. I next walked alongside the Glacier du Rhône to Andermatt; passed at the foot of St. Gotthard and visited the Devil's Bridge. On the following day I started through the valley of the Reuss, passing through Amstag and Altdorf, where William Tell was born, to Flüelen, close to the lake of the Quatre Cantons. Visited Tell's Chapel and Brunnen and back to Flüelen, where I took the steamboat to Lucerne and went to see the Lion of Thorwaldsen. The next day by coach to Zürich, where I made some sketches, and afterwards took a steamer to Rappenschwyl; thence by coach to Wesen on Lake of Wallenstadt. Proceeded to Ragatz and made an excursion to the Bains de Pfeffers. Next posted to Rorschack on Lake Constance, and down the lake by steamer to Constance. On the following day posted to Schaffhausen and saw the Falls of the Rhine. Then quitted with great regret the mountain scenery of Switzerland and posted to Freiburg, where I took the coach to Strasbourg, reaching there at half-past eleven at night, and being kept for half an hour at the gates of the town by the custom-house officers. Then proceeded by coach to Baden-Baden, Carlsruhe, and Heidelberg. The last-named town proved so interesting that I remained there for five days making sketches. Proceeded by coach to Frankfort and Mayence. I now commenced walking again with my knapsack on my back, and reached Rudesheim, where I saw the beauties of the Rhine for the first time, and crossed the river to Bingen. Next proceeded on foot to Bacharach and Pfalz, passing many old castles romantically situated on the tops of hills overlooking the river, and reached Oberwesel, with its fine castle of Schönburg. At the hotel I tried to speak German, and on asking for some wine they brought me cold meat. Continued my walk to St. Goar, and crossed the river to see the castle of Katz. Proceeded along a path beside the river to Boppart and Coblenz, where I crossed the bridge of boats to visit Ehrenbreitstein. Next continued to Andernach,

THE MARKET-PLACE, MAL

(Size 30 × 20½ *inches.)*

and then to Remagen, and finished my walking
tour at Bonn, where I took the steamer to Cologne
and posted on from there to Aix-la-Chapelle and
then to Liĕge, where I took the train—the railway
had not long been opened—to Brussels, and thence
by diligence *viâ* Valenciennes and Noyons to Paris,
reaching it after an absence of ten weeks.
Travelling in those days was not at all like what it
is at the present time. English was not understood, and having no knowledge of the German
language, I was compelled to make signs for nearly
everything I required during the three weeks I
was in Germany, especially in the Moselle district.

On my return to Paris I found that the Princess
Clémentine was staying at Neuilly, so I had to
walk there each morning to give her a drawing
lesson at eight o'clock in the morning. In order
to be there in time I was obliged to get up at six,
my brother making me a cup of tea before I
started, and I had my breakfast on my return.
This I continued to do even through the winter
months.

In 1839 I received a second silver medal at the
Exhibition of Cambrai for water-colour drawings
which I sent there. I also obtained a bronze
medal at the Rouen Exhibition. In this year

J. Mackenzie, the Treasurer of the Old Water-Colour Society, came to Paris to make some drawings for the work on Versailles, on which I was already engaged. He was commissioned to execute a few architectural subjects, chiefly interiors of the grand galleries of the Palace, whilst I drew the gardens, fountains, Trianon, and the Orangerie.

About this time *émeutes* were a frequent occurrence in Paris, and my brother and I had one or two narrow escapes as we used to run out at the sound of the *rappel* on the drums to see what would happen. It was also in this year, the tenth of my residence in Paris, that I had the honour of being introduced to the Duc d'Aumale whilst giving a lesson to the Princess at St. Cloud.

In the autumn my brother and I paid a visit to England, travelling by a new route. We took the diligence to St. Valery, and thence went by a steamer, the *Castor*, direct to London. The navigation of the Somme was very difficult, owing to the river being almost choked with sand; consequently the boats only ran for one season. On my return to Paris I received an invitation from the Comte de Noë to dinner, at which I met his son, the noted caricaturist, well known as "Cham," whose

drawings were reproduced in *Le Charivari* and
other publications. I also received commissions
from the Princess Clémentine and from the Duc de
Nemours for drawings to present to their friends.

In this year Messrs. Moon, Boys and Graves,
the publishers, had brought out a lithographic
work on Old Paris executed by Thomas Shotter
Boys, cousin to the member of the firm, and I was
asked by them to present a copy to King Louis
Philippe, which I did through the Princess. It
was graciously accepted, and shortly afterwards
a diamond ring was sent by the King to the
publishers. My friend, T. S. Boys, was terribly
disappointed, as he was the person who should have
received the present; the mistake occurred through
the publishers, and not the artist, sending the
book.

In 1840 I attended a grand representation
of Racine's play *Andromaque* at the Theatre
Français, in which Mdlle. Rachel took part. It
was followed by a comedy, in which Mdlle. Mars,
though seventy years of age, played the character
of a young girl; she had long retired from the
stage, and reappeared only for this special occasion.
It was a memorable performance, as Mdlle. Mars
was the oldest actress, and Mdlle. Rachel the

youngest in Paris at that time.   The Royal Family
were all present, and the Princess presented me
with a ticket of admission, particularly requesting
that I should make use of it myself, as they wished
to be surrounded by those who were loyal to them.

In this year I was awarded a silver medal for
my drawings exhibited at the Rouen Exhibition,
the second I had received from that town.   I was
also successful in obtaining a gold medal at the
Paris Salon.   I was to have received it from the
hands of the King, but owing to a disturbance, the
official presentation of prizes was abandoned.   I
was also fortunate enough to win a picture in
a Fine Art Lottery at Lyons.   I sold it for five
hundred francs without even seeing it.

I paid a short visit to London to judge the
effect of my own drawings on the walls of the Old
Water-Colour Society's gallery at the annual
Exhibition, and returned to Paris accompanied by
my friend Bentley.   I may mention here that on
each anniversary of the Revolution King Louis
Philippe caused it to be commemorated by three
days' fêtes.   Every kind of amusement which could
be devised was provided for the people; theatres and
cafés were open free, prizes were awarded for climbing greasy poles and other sports, including aquatic

ones on the river, and finally a grand display of fireworks in the Place de la Concorde wound up the fĕtes. All this was done by the King in order to try and please the people, in spite of which constant attempts were being made on his life. I remember on one occasion after a review, as the King, accompanied by some officers, was passing along the Boulevards, a shot was fired from a window; it fortunately missed him, but wounded several of the officers.

In the autumn of this year I made my first visit to Italy. I was accompanied for some part of the time by Forman, who had been with me two years previously on the tour through Switzerland. We left Paris by diligence for Dijon, and then crossed the Jura mountains to Geneva, where we stopped and sketched. We next passed on the left side of the lake through Lausanne and Vevey to St. Maurice, where we changed diligences and arrived at Brieg. The next day we crossed the Simplon Pass and reached Domo d'Ossola at 11 P.M. After sleeping for a few hours on a sofa we took the *malle poste* in the early morning to Arona on Lago Maggiore. Here we stayed and sketched. Afterwards crossed the lake to Angera to see the picturesque castle, and made a trip up the lake by steamer to

enjoy the scenery. On the same evening we took a
carriage to Bellinzona, and made some sketches in
the very picturesque town with its old walls and
towers before breakfast the next morning. Later
we proceeded to Lugano, passing over Mont
Cannĕro, and witnessing some splendid views on
the road. The next day we left by coach for
Como, crossed the lake in a boat, and arrived there
in the evening. On the following day we took a
steamer up the lake, which is smaller but prettier
than Maggiore, and went ashore at Bellaggio. Here,
although there was no hotel, we obtained some very
comfortable quarters and stayed the night. We
took a delightful sail up the lake, but, owing to a
contrary wind, could only reach Gravedona, where it
was impossible to stay, as every cottage was so dirty;
consequently we returned as far as Domaso. Next
day, after sailing for seven hours, we managed to
reach Cadenabbia, opposite to Bellaggio, then took
the steamer back to Como, being very much pleased
with the trip. Sketched all the next day at Como
and left in the evening for Milan in a *velociferi*,
a long vehicle holding about twenty people, and
after four hours' jolting arrived at the capital
of Lombardy, where we inspected the cathedral,
the Scala, and other fine buildings. Left Milan

PIAZZA DELLE ERBE, VERONA.

From a Pencil Drawing made in 1840.

at midnight, passing through a splendidly rich
country, and, skirting Lake Garda for some distance,
arrived at Verona in the evening, after having been
almost stifled by dust and heat. We were much
interested in this town, with whole streets of
fine palaces, intermingled with Roman and other
antiquities, the tombs of the Scaligeri, the old bridge,
and amphitheatre. Next we proceeded to Padua,
with its arcaded streets and two remarkable
churches, in one of which we saw a beautiful painting by Paul Veronese. Being anxious to arrive at
Venice, we took the *malle poste* to Mestre, where
we embarked in a gondola, traversing for several
miles over the lagoons, and arrived in the evening
at the steps of Hotel Europa, delighted with our
first view of the Queen of the Adriatic. We
stayed for ten days, seeing all the wonderful sights
and making many sketches. We left Venice with
great regret and returned to Padua, whence we
posted to Ferrara, and then on to Bologna. Here
we saw the castle of the Dukes of Ferrara, a fine
fortress, the cathedral, and the leaning tower, all of
which I sketched. The next day we started in a
vettura in company with two others for Florence,
having to be drawn by oxen at a snail's pace across
the Apennines. We slept at a solitary habitation,

Albergo del Nolta, in sight of Monte di Fo, and after two days' travelling arrived at Florence. Here we remained for four days sketching all the wonderful buildings. Forman being obliged to return to Paris, I proceeded by myself in a *vettura* to Rome. The journey took six days. Stopped the first night at Arezzo, the birthplace of Petrarch, then quitted the Tuscan States and entered those of the Pope. From the Custom-house there is a beautiful view over Lake Trasimeno, near to which Hannibal obtained a famous victory over the Romans. Arrived at Perugia on the third day and visited the cathedral; afterwards took a carriage to Assisi and saw the famous convent of St. Francis, remarkable for the three churches built one above the other. We then proceeded to Foligno, and then on to Spoleto, where I made a sketch of the town and gateway where Hannibal's progress received a check from the inhabitants. Next reached Terni, where I saw the cascade and the villa where Queen Caroline resided. Continued the journey, passing Narni, with the Roman bridge built by Augustus Cæsar, and along a splendid road across the mountains and arrived at Nepi. On the last day we crossed the Campagna, beautiful in its barrenness—no trees, no water, nor cultivation

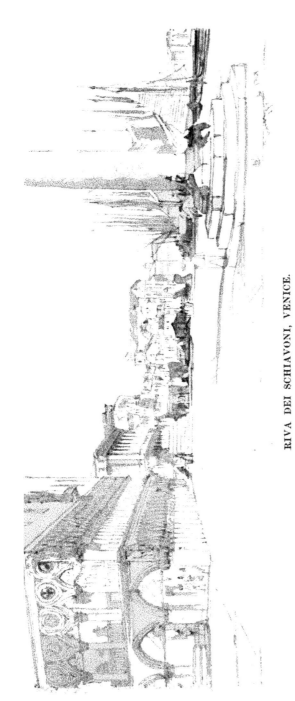

RIVA DEI SCHIAVONI, VENICE.

From a Pencil Drawing made in 1840.

of any kind, and not even a house, but how
many reflections it causes in one's mind—and
arrived at last at Rome, entering it by the Porta
del Popolo. Here I remained for ten days enjoying all the wonderful sights of that marvellous city.
Afterwards I left for Naples, stopping a night at
Terracina by the way, and reached Naples on the
following day, visiting Herculaneum and Vesuvius.
Next I took the railway to Castellamare and
walked to Torre del Greco, where I hired a
donkey and went to Castel Lettere and Gragnano ;
afterwards to Pompeii, in which place I was greatly
interested. From there I proceeded to Torre del
Greco, and then back by rail to Naples. On the
next day I took the steamer *Francisco Primo* for
Marseilles. It came on to blow so hard during the
middle of the first night that the steamer was
nearly swamped by the heavy seas, which stove
in two deck cabins, carried away some of the
boats, and filled the main cabin half full with water.
We stopped at Leghorn and Genoa, and, after
a boisterous voyage, finally reached Marseilles.
Here I remained for two days, revisiting with
pleasure many spots which I had seen during my
previous stay. I then took the diligence for
Lyons, passing along the road by Avignon and

Orange which I tramped on foot in 1836. I was obliged to stop at Lyons for two days, being unable to secure a seat on a diligence. I eventually obtained one, and after the diligence had proceeded some way on the road we were detained for six hours at one place owing to an inundation. Finally we reached Paris without any further mishap. Travelling from one place to another in those days was no easy matter, especially in Italy. The *vetturino* generally started at a very early hour in the morning, stopped during the intense heat of the day for the passengers to rest, and proceeded on its journey in the evening. All the way from Rome to Naples the *malle poste* was accompanied by a mounted guard for protection against the banditti.

Soon after my return from Italy I was commanded to take my sketches to the Tuileries, and was commissioned to make three drawings from them, one for Queen Marie Amelie, one for the Duc de Nemours, and one for Princess Clémentine; the last named shortly afterwards requested me to make two more drawings, and I was continually receiving proofs of the Princess's kindness.

At the end of this year the remains of Napoleon

RIVA DEI SCHIAVON·I, VENICE·(1894)

(*Size* 22$\frac{1}{3}$ × 15$\frac{2}{3}$ *inches.*)

were brought to France in the *Belle Poule*, a frigate commanded by Prince de Joinville, from St. Helena. They reached Paris on 14th December. It was a glorious day, but very cold. I witnessed the arrival from the garden of the Chamber of Deputies, opposite to the Pont de la Concorde, for which I had been presented with a ticket of admission by the Princess. There was an immense number of troops. The magnificent car was covered with purple crepe dotted all over with golden bees, and the horses, also draped with crepe reaching to the ground, were led by Marshals of the Army, whilst others walked beside the car holding the pall. As the procession crossed the bridge on the way to the Invalides the sun shone out, and it was a most brilliant spectacle.

In 1841 I made two large water-colour drawings from my Italian sketches for the Old Water-Colour Society's Exhibition, one of Venice, and the other of Naples from the Sea.

Many inquiries were now being made for me in London, and I was strongly advised to quit Paris and to take up my residence permanently in England. My drawings at the Old Society's Exhibition were much appreciated, and Thackeray had written two years previously in *Fraser's Magazine:* " A new painter, somewhat in the style of Harding, is Mr. Callow; and better, I think, than his master or original, whose colours are too gaudy, to my taste, and effects too glaringly theatrical "; success seemed, therefore, assured. I accordingly commenced preparations for leaving Paris by selling many of my possessions, which I had accumulated during my residence in that city for nearly twelve years. Although I had never entertained the idea of settling there for life, still when the time came I left with much regret, for the period had been passed most happily. I had here begun my career as a lad unaided, but by continued exertions and hard work had been most successful. From the small sum of twenty-five francs, which I had first deposited in the Savings Bank at the instigation of Himley, I had now fourteen thousand francs invested in the Funds. I had also made so many kind friends, and had become so well known professionally, that I was truly grieved to leave Paris, and my great grief was in severing my connection with the Royal Family, particularly the Princess Clémentine, to whom I had given drawing lessons twice a week for nearly seven years, always punctually at eight o'clock in the morning, whether at Paris, St. Cloud, or Neuilly; also Prince de Joinville, to whom I had given occasional lessons on his return from Mexico. My principal furniture, books, and prints were purchased by Baron Schweiter and other friends; the remainder I left with my brother John to furnish his apartments, as he remained in Paris working on his own account.

I finally quitted Paris on 28th March 1841, and settled in London, rather nervous as to the result, for having given up my Royal pupil as well as a good connection as a drawing-master amongst many of the old French aristocracy, I had to start afresh and practically unknown in London.

LINCOLN.

CHAPTER V

IN LONDON

DURING the first year of my residence in London I had only one pupil, Lady Beaujolois Bury, a daughter of the Earl of Charleville, but I was successful in selling a number of drawings. I resumed my acquaintance with Mr. Kalergi, who was living in the same street as myself. He was a rich Russian, having inherited about half a million of money from his father; I first met him in Paris. We frequently passed many pleasant days together.

85

Sometimes he drove me down to Richmond, where his mother was staying, and I made numerous sketches there. In fact he was most kind to me, and frequently invited me to dinner at his house. Sometimes after dinner he would send his valet to secure a box at the Opera. Arriving there, Kalergi would be amused for a time, but would often soon tire of it and we would return before the finish to his house, when he would play all the airs to which he had just listened. He was a clever pianist, and I remember on one occasion after having heard the 'Stabat Mater' for the first time he played it all from memory. During the year many of my old friends from Paris, including Comte de Noë, Comte Stackleberg, Baron Schweitzer, and others, called to see me at my studio.

In the autumn I made a sketching tour in Normandy, accompanied by Bentley. We visited St. Malo and Avranches. From the latter place we went in a country cart to St. Malo. On our complaining of the roughness of the road and the jolting of the cart the driver gravely informed us that it was the same road the great Napoleon had traversed, which, however, did not console us for the bumping we received during the drive. We next proceeded to Caen, where we took the

LONDON FROM HOLLY LODGE, HIGHGATE (1

(Size 12¾ x 18¼ inches)

steamer to Havre, and afterwards walked along the coast to Dieppe, thence through Abbeville to Paris, and returned from there direct to London.

About this time Adelaide Kemble made her first appearance on the stage of Covent Garden Theatre in *Norma.* I went to hear the Opera, and was agreeably surprised to find an accomplished

DARTMOUTH.

artiste instead of the nervous young singer whom I had heard some years previously in her own home at Paris. She was perfect in her character and sang divinely. She afterwards became Mrs. Sartoris, and relinquished the stage.

During the next year, 1842, my pupils increased in number. Amongst others were Lady Stratford de Redcliffe and her family, who came to receive lessons before departing for Constantinople to join his lordship, who was British Ambassador there. Miss Crewe, a sister of Lord Crewe, was also a pupil, and I went to give her some lessons at Madeley Manor, in Staffordshire, the seat of Mrs. Cunliffe Offley, the aunt of Miss Crewe, with whom she was staying. I unfortunately caught a severe cold on the last day of my visit through sitting on the damp grass, so I decided to go to the South Coast to recuperate. It entailed a tedious journey by coach, passing through Bristol and Exeter to Plymouth, whence I made a short sketching tour to Dartmouth, Torquay, Teignmouth, Lyme Regis, and Corfe Castle.

I had now accumulated sufficient money to purchase the lease of my house, 20 Charlotte Street, Portland Place, where I resided for some years, Bentley sharing part of it until my marriage. My pupils became still more numerous. Amongst them was Lord Dufferin, who, however, was more interested in chemistry than drawing, so much so that his mother, one of the beautiful Sheridan sisters, told me that she was in constant fear lest he should blow up their house. I lost sight of my pupil for many years, but followed his brilliant career with great interest, especially during the time he was Viceroy of India. Shortly before his

ENTRANCE TO THE PORT OF HA

(Size 20¼ × 14 inches.)

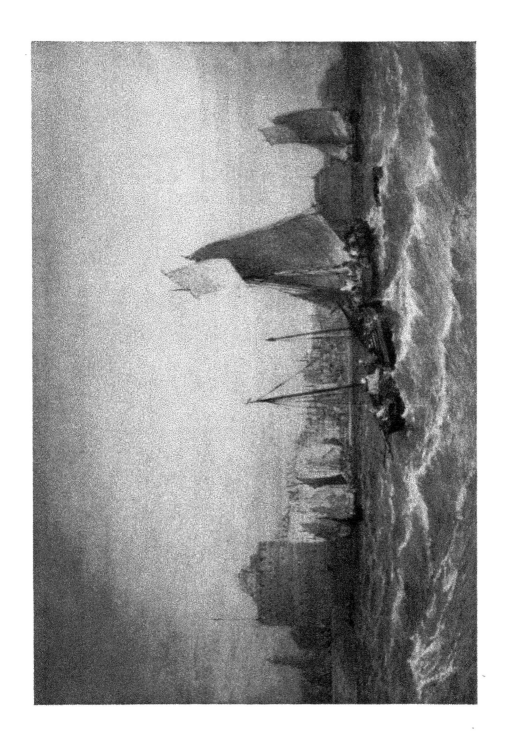

death I wrote to condole with him on the loss of his eldest son, who was killed during the Boer War. He sent a charming letter to me in reply, saying he often noticed my name in newspapers, and in addition was pleasantly reminded of me by a lovely work of mine hanging on the wall in his drawing-room.

In 1843 I exhibited a painting of the " Port of Havre" at the Old Society. It was purchased by Mr. W. Prinsep as a gift for a distinguished Indian, Dwarkanath Tagore, as it represented the place from which he embarked for England. Mr. Prinsep also gave me a commission to paint a view of Dover, being the spot at which this Indian had first set foot in England. These drawings were subsequently sent to him in India.

I paid a second visit to Madeley Manor, and whilst there saw Crewe Hall, the country seat of Lord Crewe, a lovely place full of fine pictures and antiquities. It was shortly afterwards burnt down, and the picture gallery was seriously damaged by fire. From Madeley I proceeded to Liverpool, and took the steamer for Glasgow, calling at Douglas, in the Isle of Man. It was a lovely trip up the river Clyde, and I was fortunate in seeing the charming scenery in fine weather.

12

From Glasgow I took the train to Edinburgh, a city glorious in position and effect. The mists were rather against sketching, for I had to go to the hills three times to obtain a general view of the city before I was successful. After spending some days sketching I went by coach to Melrose, Jedburgh, Berwick, Bamborough Castle, Alnwick, and

CHATSWORTH.

Durham; then by an omnibus from Catterick Bridge to Richmond, and back to London. Travelling by coach in these days was a great pleasure. Stopping at the principal towns, one was welcomed at the inns by the landlords, and was served as travellers never are and never will be again. During this little tour I made many sketches, from which I executed later finished water-colour paintings.

In the month of December I received a com-

LA GRANDE PLACE, BRU

MARKET DAY (1891)

(Size 12¾ x 18⅜ inches)

mission from the Duke of Devonshire to make two drawings of Chatsworth for Queen Victoria's album, one of the house from the garden, and the other a view from the conservatory—two points of interest which Her Majesty had greatly admired during her visit to Chatsworth with Prince Consort. The Duke gave instructions to his head gardener, Mr. Joseph Paxton, afterwards knighted for his services in connection with the great Exhibition of 1851, to look after me, and having to work in the open air during bitterly cold weather, a furnace was placed near me, so that I could warm myself, and a manservant was deputed to wait on me. When the drawings were finished the Duke came to see them at my studio, and he was so pleased with them that he increased the price originally stipulated.

In August 1844, after an exceptionally busy time in London, I was tempted to revisit the Rhine and the Moselle, so I crossed to Calais, and went by diligence to Dunkirk, from there through Bruges and Malines, making a number of sketches at both places, to Cologne, and then up the Rhine by steamer to Coblenz. After staying there for a few days I started in a very small steamer up the Moselle, and landed at Carden on a lovely evening. The next morning I proceeded by boat to Cochem, where I remained for several days sketching. The proprietor of the hotel spoke French, and very obligingly walked out with me to point out the principal objects of interest,

EISENACH.

including Schloss Elz. I next went to Trarbach, a secluded spot with no travellers, and with few means of communication with other places. I made a number of sketches in this charmingly picturesque old town, and on revisiting Trarbach, seventeen years afterwards, I learnt that about the year 1860 the principal street, with its quaint buildings, which I had sketched, had been burnt down. From Trarbach I visited the pretty village of Alf, where the river runs round a promontory, on the top of which is the ruined castle of Marienburg; then proceeded by Berncastel to Trèves. The three weeks which I spent alone beside the banks of the Moselle were most enjoyable, the only drawback being my utter ignorance of the German language. Whilst on my way to Trèves I saw an immense number of pilgrims, headed by priests and banners, both going to and returning from that city, where the Holy Coat, without seam, which had been lost for upwards of fifty years, had just been found, built up, I was informed, in a wall of the cathedral. It was on view to the faithful, and thousands of pilgrims were flocking day and night from Bavaria, Saxony, and other countries in order to behold it. I was told that I had arrived too late to see it, but a small tip was sufficient to open sesame. The coat was displayed in a glass case, which I was not allowed to approach nearer than one hundred yards. The niece of the Archbishop of Trèves was the only one allowed to kiss the hem of the garment; she had been lame for many years, so report ran, and on kissing it she was immediately cured, throwing away her crutches and dancing for joy.

In spite of the rapidity of the Upper Moselle, a boat started for Thionville, in which I took a place; but the current being unusually swift, it was unable to reach that place, so I landed and took the coach to Paris, where I stayed for a week with my brother John, and then returned to London. In these years a great difficulty was experienced in leaving France. It was absolutely necessary to have a passport, and one had to attend the Bureau de Passeport, where full particulars of one's height, colour of the eyes, length of nose, etc., were carefully noted. The passport had afterwards to be presented at the British Embassy to be viséed by the Ambassador, which took three days, and for which a charge of five francs was made. It had also to be countersigned and registered at the port on quitting France. One of the earliest which I possess is quite a curiosity.

The year 1845 was one of considerable moment to me, for I became engaged to one of my pupils, Miss Harriet Anne Smart, a niece of Sir George Smart, the Queen's organist, and sister to Henry Smart, the organist and composer. She was also a clever musician, being an excellent pianist and

THE CATHEDRAL, ANTW

(Size 26 x 19 inches)

vocalist, and was besides a good linguist. At the
wish of her relations we waited a year before being
married.

During the summer I made a sketching tour
in Holland. I went by steamer to Rotterdam, and

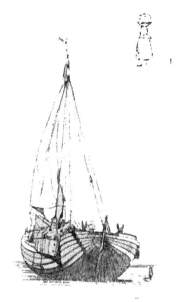

SCHEVENINGEN.

then to The Hague, where I made the acquaintance
of a gentleman, who obtained for me an invitation
to an evening party at the house of a Dutch family.
It was rather a formal but interesting affair, with
music and conversation, the latter being in French.
From The Hague I visited Scheveningen, where
I obtained some good sketches of Dutch fishing-

boats, and then proceeded by diligence to Delft, Leyden, and Haarlem.   These places were exceedingly dull, there being very few people to be seen in the streets, and at the last-named town I was the only traveller at the hotel, where I dined alone in a room capable of holding five hundred persons. I next took up my quarters at Amsterdam, which was more lively, as it was fair time and there were plenty of amusements, besides, I had an opportunity of seeing Rembrandt's glorious paintings.   I afterwards had a most interesting trip by steamer through the canals to Antwerp, and from there I returned to England.

I had in my younger days been a great smoker, but when I commenced to receive lady pupils I could only indulge in a pipe during the evenings, and now on the approach of my marriage I decided to give up the habit entirely.   I practically ceased smoking from this date, and have never resumed it.

In the spring of the following year, 1846, I was busily superintending alterations and the decoration of my house in Charlotte Street previous to my marriage with Miss Smart, which ceremony took place at St. Margaret's Church, Westminster, in the presence of a large number of relations and friends. We started on our honeymoon to Ramsgate, and

OLD BRIDGE, NUREMBERG

(Size 14¾ x 10¾ inches)

on the next day crossed to Ostend. Another pupil of mine happened to be married on the same day as ourselves, and we, curiously, met on board the steamer. I had to look after both the brides during the crossing, as the other husband disappeared shortly after the steamer started. Our honeymoon lasted ten weeks, during which time we went up the Rhine and across Switzerland to Venice. At Cologne we saw the cathedral before its completion. The crane at the top of the unfinished tower had been removed from that position, and immediately afterwards, so it was said, a terrific storm did an immense amount of damage, and the priests, looking upon it as a judgment, caused the crane to be replaced on the tower, where it remained till the Emperor William I. of Germany had the cathedral completed. I was at first disappointed with Nuremberg, but on looking round I found many capital subjects. The picturesque buildings were, however, very difficult to sketch, owing to the amount of detail; in fact I experienced the same difficulty in all the old German towns. At Munich we saw an interesting fair, with Tyrolean peasants in their national costumes. I made many sketches of them. We passed lovely scenery on our way to Innsbrück, and on arriving at the

Austrian frontier all our luggage was examined in the open air. The scenery of the Alps from Innsbrück is charming, and we especially enjoyed the view looking down the winding river from the bridge by moonlight. The old city of Trent is also beautifully situated, and I found many subjects there for my pencil. We next proceeded to the beautiful city of Verona, with its picturesque old buildings and its wonderful market-place. To my mind it ranks next to Venice in point of interest. The market-place was a great source of interest to us; Italian ladies with black veils wandering about and making purchases at the stalls covered with huge white umbrellas made an animated scene. From Verona we went to Vicenza, where we took the train to Venice, and rowed up the Grand Canal to Hotel Europa late in the evening. The calm and quietude were heavenly after several weeks' of travelling by diligence and rail. The city at this period belonged to Austria, and Austrian soldiers were to be seen everywhere. The Austrians and Venetians kept quite apart; each had their separate cafés on either side of the Piazza. Still it was Venice, the same as of old.

On our return journey we arrived at Flüelen in torrents of rain; found the church surrounded by water, and were obliged to enter our hotel by means of planks. Lucerne was also flooded on our arrival, and we were unable to go to the Schwan Hotel, where I stayed on my previous visit, on account of the lower part of the house being under water. We arrived home on the 12th September after an enjoyable trip, which was, however, to some extent marred by my wife's delicate health.

I now settled down to serious work both in teaching and making drawings for the Old Society's Exhibitions, and owing to my wife's ill-health our gaieties were few. Amongst my pupils were Mr. Owen Stanley and his sister; their father was the Bishop of Norwich, and President of the Linnean Society. I often attended meetings and soirées at his house in connection with the Society, which were deeply interesting to me.

In 1847 I paid a visit to Mr. Geoffrey Windus at Tottenham to see his remarkable collection of Turner drawings, in addition to other beautiful paintings which adorned the walls of his rooms. I was so much impressed with the loveliness of Turner's work that I can even now recall them to my memory. The sales at the Old Society's Exhibition, for the first time since my election in 1838, were very bad, which caused me much dis-

appointment, but fortunately I was most successful with my teaching, having almost more pupils
than I was able to properly superintend.   I also
painted a few small pictures in oils, which I sent
to the British Institution in the following year, and
continued to do so annually until the Exhibitions
were discontinued.   In 1848 I was again disappointed in the sales at the Old Society, but this
was fully compensated for by the good news which
Bentley brought to me one evening, announcing
that I had been elected a full member of the
Society of Painters in Water Colours.   The great
ambition of my life was now attained.   How proud
was I to think that for the future I was to be included in a body of celebrated men to whom as a boy
I had looked up with an admiration approaching
to awe, and to belong to the Society and home of
water-colour paintings.   I wonder how many of the
younger generation have appreciated the honour of
membership of this famous Society to the same
degree as I have done, and still continue to do.

In the autumn of this year my wife and I made
a tour to Tewkesbury, Worcester, and Hereford,
at which places I found plenty of subjects to
sketch.   A small painting of a view in the first-
named town was purchased at the Old Society's

Exhibition by Charles Dickens for eight guineas, and at the sale of his effects after his death this drawing fetched fifty-four guineas. We continued our journey by coach to Ross and Monmouth, visiting all the beautiful places along the river Wye, including Goodrich Court, belonging to Colonel Meyrick, with its famous collection of armour. Whilst we were at Abergavenny there was a Cymrygyddion fête, at which there was a harpist competition. "Poor Marianne" was the piece selected to be played, and one of the competitors insisted on playing it with sixteen variations. On being told by the judges that six would be sufficient, he said that unless he was allowed to play it all through as he had learnt it, he would fail entirely, so he was allowed to have his way, and bored the audience excessively.

On our return to London I accompanied Bentley to a meeting of the members of the Old Society. It was my first attendance, and I was introduced by him to those present. The number of members at that time was four and twenty. At a subsequent meeting during the presidency of Copley Fielding, at which I was present, Evans, "of Eton," put forward a motion limiting the number of works to be sent by each member for Exhibition. Copley Fielding, who always contributed many drawings, felt that the proposal was levelled at him, and was much pained by it. He appealed to William Hunt, the fruit and flower painter, for his opinion. The latter, who was of small stature and slightly deformed, and who had a very gentle manner, said that he should be sorry not to be able to send any number of drawings he might be able to paint, without limit. Whereupon Evans withdrew his motion, and added that he had no intention of hurting the feelings of the President or of any of the members. I rarely saw David Cox, except on "touching-up" days, as he was then living in Birmingham. He was a very jovial fellow. In the Gallery Cox once remarked that he had never received a hundred guineas for any one drawing. He was overheard by a stranger, who, addressing Cox, said, "You shall not state that again, for I will give you that amount for the picture hanging on the wall." It was the well-known "Welsh Funeral at Bettws-y-Coed." At one of the Exhibitions a bright drawing of mine, full of Italian sunshine, was placed on the line next to another by Peter De Wint, which, although very powerful in colour, was dark in tone. He considered that mine placed his at a

INNSBRUCK
From an Oil Painting

(*Size* 22 × 29½ *inches.*)

disadvantage, and suggested to me that I should subdue my drawing by placing a warm tint all over it. Needless to say my brother artists advised me to take no notice of the suggestion, which, if it had been carried out, would have ruined my work.

It was about this period that a gentleman called upon me one day, and inquired if I could make a drawing of a bird's-eye view of Dover. As I knew the town well, I replied in the affirmative. He then desired to know if I could also do another of the Pyramids. At first I expressed a doubt, but when he offered to supply me with a map of the Nile I consented to do my best, and he gave me a commission for the two drawings. When they were ready the gentleman called again and took them away. The matter passed out of my mind until some weeks afterwards, on looking at a copy of the *Illustrated London News*, I saw a print of a flying machine passing over my view of Dover, and a second print of the machine arriving at the Pyramids.

In 1849 I made a sketching tour in the west of Scotland, arriving at Glasgow whilst the Queen and Prince Albert were there, and afterwards visiting the Kyles of Bute and Inveraray, where my wife and I stayed for a month in most primitive but comfortable quarters, being waited upon by a maid without shoes or stockings.

During the next year I was much occupied in oil painting, sending " A View of Bologna " and " The Trongate, Glasgow," to the British Institution, and "Nuremberg" and "Fĕcamp" (a water-colour) to the Royal Academy. I also contributed twenty drawings to the Old Society, and was fortunate in selling all of them. It was a rule of the Society at this time that the price of the drawings should not include frames, which were much more expensive than they are now, and purchasers had the option of buying the drawings framed or unframed. In the earlier days, prior to my election, the Society, in order to induce members to make large and important drawings, provided frames and plate glass complete in which members might place their works. This system did not answer for long, and soon after I became an Associate it was given up. A lottery was held for the remaining frames, and I was successful in gaining one of them. The Society held a very high position in those days. The Exhibitions were well attended, and on private view days the gallery was crowded, visitors even waiting outside before the doors were opened in order to obtain an early admission. The Society was also in such a prosperous state that members received fees for attending meetings and for hanging the drawings for the Exhibitions. The meetings were consequently well attended, and a very pleasant time was frequently spent discussing art with my fellow-members.

My brother John, who had joined the New Society in 1845, left it three years later and became an Associate of the Old Society in this year, 1849. He continued his connection with it until his death in 1878.

During the summer we went to a centenary commemoration of the death of the great musical composer Bach, at which my brother-in-law, Henry Smart, conducted.

Afterwards we made a very interesting excursion through Belgium for the purpose of sketching. We visited Lille, Courtrai, Tournai, Bruges, Ghent, and Antwerp. At all these towns I had little time for seeing the sights, as I found so many architectural subjects admirably suited for my pencil.

During the year of the great Exhibition our travels were confined to Lincolnshire and Norfolk, and we went, amongst other interesting places, to Sudbrook Hall, in order to see the celebrated

14

Ellison Collection of Water-Colour Drawings, now in the Victoria and Albert Museum.

I was present at the Gallery, in 1852, when Queen Victoria, Prince Albert, and their two eldest children, accompanied by the Duchess of

ANTWERP.

Cambridge, visited it.   Each member had the honour of being separately presented to the Royal Family.   The Queen, after looking round the gallery, graciously came up to me and said, "You are, I think, Mr. Callow.   I have heard of you from the Princess Clémentine, and of your teaching

THE BELFRY A

(*Size* 25½ ×

drawing to the members of King Louis Philippe's family in Paris." Her Majesty also inquired if I was settled in England, and asked me many questions relative to my painting. Prince Albert also had a long conversation with me respecting art, and wanted to know whether the drawings would not be improved by white mounts, when I explained that the drawings were framed close up, in accordance with the rules of the Society, to prove that they could stand the gilt as well as oil paintings. Both the Queen and the Prince purchased one of my drawings, and out of the twenty which I contributed to this Exhibition I was fortunate in selling nineteen.

In August we made a tour in Germany, starting from Cologne to Düsseldorf, where an Exhibition was being held; to Hanover, where I made sketches of the Rathhaus; to Brunswick, seeing the tombs of the reigning family, where an attendant placed in my hands the dried heart of the Duke who lost his life in trying to rescue some lions during an inundation; and then to Leipsic, where we saw Bach's monument, and to Dresden with its numerous museums. We travelled home by Cassel and Frankfort.

After the Revolution of 1848 King Louis

Philippe and his family were obliged to flee from
France. They took up their residence in exile at
Claremont, near Esher, which Queen Victoria had
placed at their disposal. In the beginning of the
year 1853 I was summoned to Claremont to renew
the drawing lessons to the Prince de Joinville and
the Princess Clémentine. On arriving there the
Queen, Marie Amelie, seized both my hands and
began speaking to me in broken English, but she
was reminded by her son that I spoke French
fluently, when she exclaimed, " Il me fait un plaisir
de vous voir. Ah ! ça me rappelle le bon vieux
temps." Both my pupils had married since I last
saw them in Paris. The Princess had become the
Duchess of Saxe-Coburg, and the Prince de Joinville
with pride showed me his children, mounting them
on chairs to do so. The drawing lessons continued
until the spring, when the Princess returned to
Germany.

In the early autumn I visited Richmond in
Yorkshire, and made numerous excursions for the
purpose of sketching, and afterwards went to
Manchester to see the Art Treasures Exhibition,
and then to Chester, a delightfully interesting city,
with endless new objects for my pencil. In the
next year, 1854, I made a tour in Normandy,

**ST. MARY'S CHURCH, RICHMOND, YORKSHIRE
BEFORE RESTORATION**

(Size 20½ x 13¼ *inches*)

accompanied as usual by my wife; we went *viâ* Dieppe, taking the diligence to Lisieux, Caen, and Havre, and then by steamer up the Seine to Rouen. On return to England I was shocked to hear of the death of my old friend and fellow - pupil Charles Bentley, from cholera, after only a few hours' illness. It was a great grief to me, as he had been a true

DIEPPE.

companion from the earliest period of our acquaintance when we worked together under the Fieldings.

During these years I was still very successful in selling my drawings at the Society's Exhibitions, besides receiving numerous commissions. I was also enabled to raise my prices, and I received one hundred and twenty guineas for a drawing of Venice at the Liverpool Exhibition.

DURHAM.

CHAPTER VI

AT GREAT MISSENDEN

LONDON did not suit my wife's health, and for some years we had been in the habit of taking apartments from time to time at Reigate and other places, I travelling up to town two or three times a week to give my lessons. We, however, considered that it would be much more satisfactory to have a cottage of our own in the country, so on one dark November morning my brother John and I started to look at one, of which we had heard,

111

in Great Missenden parish. We left Euston Station at six o'clock, travelling third class in a truck without seats or covering of any description, and after a tedious journey, the train being shunted into sidings several times to allow fast ones to pass, we reached Berkhampstead; from there we walked ten miles through Chesham to Great Missenden. We found the cottage on the top of the Chiltern Hills, one mile and a half from the village. It was a most rural spot, far away from civilisation, and there was a good orchard and three fields, with some beautiful old trees, attached to the cottage. The place with its surroundings appealed to me so greatly that I at once entered into preliminary arrangements with the owner for the purchase of it. After having some tea at a small inn close by, my brother and I walked back to Berkhampstead and took a slow train back to London, arriving home very tired after a long day. Early in the following spring, 1855, I completed the purchase of the property, and we went down to take possession of it, arriving in deep snow. We were greatly surprised to hear the church bells ringing, which we soon learnt was done to welcome us to the neighbourhood. Of course this meant a silver key to the ringers.

We were enchanted with our new home and the neighbourhood. At that time the commons were unenclosed and covered with gorse, which when in flower was most picturesque. There were lovely drives in all directions, and Hampden House, the seat of the Earl of Buckinghamshire, famed for its woods of beech trees, Chequers Court, the property of the descendants of Oliver Cromwell, and other historical houses were within easy reach.

Soon after our arrival at Great Missenden I was grieved by the death of Copley Fielding at Worthing. It was said that he never recovered from a shock caused by the death of his favourite daughter. He was a gentle, kind, and amiable man, and most courteous in his manner; he was very industrious both in teaching and painting, and for twenty-five years was a most excellent President of the Old Society, at whose exhibitions his drawings were always a great attraction. I remember his saying that he had never received a hundred guineas for any drawing which he had made, yet in 1872 I saw one of his drawings realise seven hundred guineas at the famous Gillett sale at Christie's sale-rooms.

It was during the year 1855 I learnt that the

15

Professorship of drawing at the Military Academy at Addiscombe had become vacant, but being too much occupied to undertake the duties myself, I advised my brother John to apply for the post. He was successful in obtaining it, and continued to hold it until the Academy was removed to Woolwich, when he retired and accepted a commutation. A few years later he was given a similar position at Woolwich, and after a time a military professor was appointed in his place and he received a further commutation.

In the next year, 1856, we made a charming trip, accompanied by friends, to Tours and Nantes, and thence down beside the river Loire to Blois. In the following year we went to Scotland, visiting Edinburgh, Stirling, and Aberdeen, where I sketched the Brig of Balgownie. In the autumn a dinner took place in commemoration of the fiftieth anniversary of the foundation of the Old Water-Colour Society, but owing to a dense fog I was unable to attend it.

In February 1858 I went up to town to attend a meeting of the Old Society, at which John Lewis, who had succeeded Copley Fielding in the office of President, resigned all connection with the Society. He was anxious to become associated with the Royal

TOURS

(*Size* 10½ x 19½, *section taken* 10½ ✗ 17½ *inches*)

Academy, and in accordance with its rules at that time no candidate belonging to any other Society of painters was eligible for election. Lewis was elected an Associate of the Royal Academy twelve months later. In the summer we went to Leeds to be present at the inauguration of the great organ in the Town Hall; it had been designed by my brother-in-law, Henry Smart, and he gave a magnificent performance upon it. Afterwards we paid a visit to friends in Lincolnshire, and later proceeded to Richmond in Yorkshire, where we greatly enjoyed some exquisite drives in the neighbourhood. Lady Zetland, on learning that I was staying near by, invited me to Aske Hall, and I received a commission from her for several drawings.

On our return to town I found it necessary to consult Mr. Cæsar Hawkins, the celebrated surgeon, about a small wen on my cheek, and he advised an operation, which took place under chloroform a few days later. As the wound healed but slowly I was obliged to wear a bandage over it, and was ordered to Folkestone for a change of air. Whilst there I received a letter from Lady Anthony de Rothschild requesting me to give some lessons in drawing to her and her youngest daughter at

Aston Clinton. I accordingly returned home and presented myself for the first lesson, when Lady Rothschild informed me that I should be taken for a Crimean hero on account of the bandage over my cheek. Shortly afterwards I was asked to visit Mentmore to give lessons to the Baroness Meyer de Rothschild, which I did for some time. In the spring of the next year, 1859, my wife and I, accompanied by two nieces, daughters of Henry Smart, went to a ball at Mentmore, where I met my old pupil, the Princess Clémentine. It was a most gorgeous affair, everything being carried out in royal style, and our party did not arrive home until 4.30 A.M., to the accompaniment of the singing of birds.

Having now passed five years at the cottage, we had become greatly attached to the place ; besides, my wife's health had considerably improved in the bracing atmosphere. She was greatly interested in the welfare of the cottagers, who were sadly ignorant, being unable either to read or write. All the women, girls, and boys were occupied in straw plaiting, and the only school was kept by a dame, who taught nothing but plaiting, so my wife started a small school for the benefit of the women and girls, she herself at first teaching them reading and writing; but afterwards we engaged a mistress for the purpose and converted a cottage, which I had bought, into a school-house. As our own cottage needed much repair, we found that it would be better to pull it down entirely and erect a new house in its place. This we decided to do, and rented another cottage with stables and an excellent orchard for sixteen pounds a year, in which to store our furniture and to use on flying visits to see the progress made in the building of the house. In these days the usual mode of getting to London was by a coach which started from Wendover and passed Great Missenden at 7.30 A.M., reaching the Old Bell Inn, Holborn, shortly after midday. It left on the return journey at 3 P.M., arriving at Great Missenden about eight o'clock in the evening. This coach ride through Chalfont St. Giles and Uxbridge was very enjoyable in the summer-time, the scenery being pretty most of the way. I, however, in order to give my lessons used to ride my grey mare to Berkhampstead, and then to take the train to town, returning in the evening by the same route. This I did three times a week, occasionally varying it by driving to Berkhampstead, during the London season for many years. Although we lived the greater part of the year at Great

Missenden I still kept on the house in Charlotte Street, where I gave my lessons until 1860, when we changed into another residence in Osnaburgh Terrace, near Regent's Park.

At the Old Society's Exhibition in this year *The Times* specially praised my drawings, stating, "It is long since we have seen any work of William Callow as impressive and finely conceived as his 'Castle of the Wartburg' (159), as picturesque as his 'Old Houses at Brunswick' (72), or as placid and serene as his 'Summer Evening on the Avon at Evesham' (257)." The Queen and Prince Consort, accompanied by the Princess Alice, visited the Exhibition, and I was specially sought out for notice. Holman Hunt's painting of "Finding the Saviour in the Temple" was exhibited in Bond Street at this time, and caused considerable sensation. The model for the figure of our Saviour was young Mr. Cyril Flower, who afterwards married Sir Anthony de Rothschild's eldest daughter, and became Lord Battersea.

My wife's mother, Mrs. Smart, whose health had been failing for some time, died at Watford, where she was staying, on the 9th of July, and, in accordance with a wish which she had expressed, Henry Smart and I made arrangements for her burial at Great Missenden. At the funeral an unfortunate accident occurred; the hill down to the churchyard being very steep, and there being but little space for carriages to turn, the first mourning coach, in which Henry Smart and myself were seated, upset at the church door. We were, however, hauled out through the window, shaken, but unhurt.

In the autumn we took a trip from Coblenz up the Moselle, going over nearly the same route as I did alone in 1844, and I was horrified to find that Trarbach was an entirely new place with bright green doors and brass knockers. Old Trarbach, with its picturesque streets, old houses, and the beautiful old tower, had disappeared, being destroyed by fire shortly after my visit. The sketches which I then made consequently became very valuable to me.

In June 1861 we took up our residence in our new house, which we named "The Firs," on account of the number of fir trees surrounding it. It is situated midway between the villages of Great Missenden and Lee, so we attended the churches of both parishes for worship. At this time the church at the former place had pews in the galleries very like boxes in a theatre, and the service was

most primitive.   There was no choir, and the music
consisted of a clarionet and a violin.   The tuning
up of the latter was a most wonderful performance.
One hymn was a particular favourite, "Travelling
through the wilderness."   This line was repeated
so frequently that we often wondered if the wilderness would ever be got through.   A few years
later matters improved, and an organ was acquired.
The church, however, was in a very dilapidated
state, and there being no vestry, the clergyman was
obliged to put on his gown at the reading-desk
before ascending the pulpit to preach.   Later my
wife made an appeal for money, and got up a
bazaar in order to supply funds for erecting a new
building.   Plans were designed by our friend, Mr.
Augustus Frère, who had built our house, but the
Bishop of Oxford (Wilberforce) disapproved of
them, and wanted the matter to be placed in the
hands of the diocesan architect.   To this we
objected, and for a time the project hung fire, but
eventually the Bishop, finding that we were
obdurate, gave his consent to Mr. Frère's plans.
Some years afterwards I met Bishop Wilberforce
at a déjeûner.   He was extremely civil and full of
good stories.

I well remember in the year 1862 going to hear

THE FIRS, GREAT MISSENDEN.

From a Photograph by Wm. Coles, Watford.

Charles Dickens give a reading of his *Christmas Carol.* It was most impressive. Suddenly covering his face with his hands at a most affecting part, he reduced all his audience to tears. I was never so touched by any reading as that of Dickens, which was distinguished by a great simplicity of manner.

In the following year I attended a grand reception given in honour of Grant and Speke for their discovery of the source of the Nile, at the rooms of the Royal Geographical Society, of which I was a fellow. The rooms were crowded, and the enthusiasm of those outside the building was so great that a number of windows were broken in the endeavour to hear Speke's lecture. He spoke until past midnight, his audience being spell-bound. I enjoyed it immensely. Ever since my boyhood, when I had read Denham and Clapperton's *Travels to Timbuctoo*, I had been always greatly interested with everything connected with the dark continent of Africa.

After the death of the Prince Consort, which had recently occurred, I thought that some drawings of Coburg, Rheinhardtsbrunn, and other royal palaces with which he had been connected would be of interest to the public, so I wrote to the Duchess

16

Augustus of Saxe-Coburg, formerly my pupil,
Princess Clémentine, asking her to obtain per-

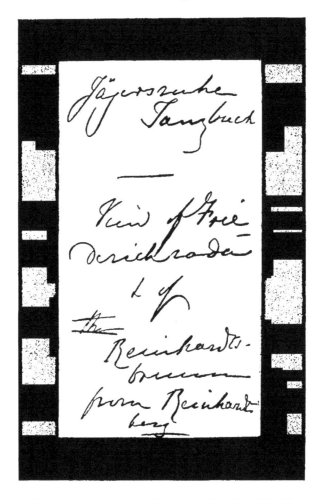

FACSIMILE OF NOTES MADE BY QUEEN VICTORIA.

mission for me to sketch at these places, which she
readily obtained. In August 1863 we arrived at
Coburg and put up at the Grüner Baum Hotel

in the market-place, opposite to a fountain in which fish were kept.   The peasants fetching water

FACSIMILE OF NOTES MADE BY QUEEN VICTORIA.

and pigeons flying about made it an animated scene from our windows.   On learning that the Royal Family had arrived at Coburg, I at once

left my card at the Palace, and on the same evening I received a command to go there the next
morning.   I was welcomed by the Duke and
Duchess and their daughters, to whom I showed
my sketches.   The Duchess requested me to leave
them with her, as she was going to Rosenau to
see Queen Victoria, who had arrived there, and on
the next day I was commanded by the Queen to
present myself at the Château at eleven o'clock on
the following morning.   I accordingly went, and
found the Queen under a tent in the garden.   I was
duly presented, but Her Majesty graciously said, "I
remember Mr. Callow perfectly."   After looking
through my sketches, and expressing her admiration for them, the Queen told me of a number of
places of interest which I ought to visit and
sketch.   I ventured to tell Her Majesty that I
did not speak German, and I was afraid that I
should not remember the names which she had
mentioned, whereupon she graciously offered to
make a note of them for me, and taking two half-
sheets of deep mourning-paper, wrote down the
names.   These two pieces of notepaper I have
always cherished in recollection of this very pleasing interview which I had with the Queen.

Shortly afterwards the Crown Prince and

Princess of Prussia arrived at Coburg on a visit to the Duke and Duchess, and I received another command to take my sketches to the Palace for inspection. The Prince and Princess received me most kindly, and after admiring my sketches

RHEINHARDTSBRUNN.

and talking on various subjects, the Princess gave me an invitation to Potsdam, which was warmly supported by the Prince, who said, "Do come, Mr. Callow, and the Princess will show you all there is to be seen." I accepted the invitation, and was informed that quarters would be reserved for me at the Einsiedler Hotel.

On leaving Coburg we visited Rheinhardtsbrunn
and Gotha, making numerous sketches at both
places.   From the latter town we took the railway
to Potsdam, and went to the hotel, as previously
arranged.   I at once informed the Princess of my
arrival at Potsdam, and received a command to be
at the Palace at 8 A.M. on the following morning.
This necessitated an early rising, as the Palace was
half an hour's drive from the hotel.   On my
reaching the Palace I was told by a footman
that I was one minute late, and on being conducted
into the presence of the Princess I found her
waiting for me, and I apologised for the delay.
We then proceeded to look for a subject to sketch,
and found a suitable one just outside the grounds.
We had not been working long before a lady-in-
waiting came and informed the Princess that
breakfast was ready.   They left me busy sketching
and returned to the Palace.   Presently a man-
servant brought me my breakfast, consisting of
cutlets, claret, coffee, etc., on a tray, and at the
same time stated that Her Royal Highness
desired me to dine with her at three o'clock.
He told me that it was necessary to put on evening
dress, but on my explaining that my clothes were
at the hotel and that there would be no time to go

and fetch them, he said under these circumstances
that the Princess would excuse morning dress. After
breakfast was over the Princess, accompanied by
two of her ladies-in-waiting, Countess Bruhl and
the Countess Hohenloe, returned, and as soon as I
had finished my sketch, carriages were ordered to
take us to Sans Souci, the Princess driving,
accompanied by one lady, in a carriage with four
horses, whilst I followed with the other lady in a
carriage and pair. On reaching Sans Souci we
alighted to sketch, and before returning to Potsdam
we mounted to the top of the Belvidere to see the
view of the surrounding country. On arriving back
at the Palace a man-servant showed me into a room
upstairs, and told me that I had three minutes to
get ready for dinner. I rapidly washed my hands,
and on descending found the Princess and her
ladies already dressed and on the Terrace waiting
for dinner to be announced. We were a party of
six. I sat opposite to the Princess, who had a
gentleman on each side of her, and the two ladies-
in-waiting sat on either side of me. After dinner,
during which the Princess chatted pleasantly with
every one, we drove to the Ile des Faisans, which
was in a narrow river, and had to be reached by a
punt. After the ladies had got into the punt, I

followed, laden with sketch-books, etc., and one of the ladies punted to the island. On reaching it they landed, and the last one hastily pushed the punt back into the river, and they all walked away laughing merrily, leaving me standing up in the punt with my arms full of impedimenta. There was nothing for it but to put down my burden and to punt to the bank. Eventually I landed and caught up the Princess and her ladies. In the evening I was driven back to the hotel, accompanied by the Countess Bruhl, who bore a gift of some flowers from the Princess to my wife, also an invitation for her to go to the Palace on the next day.

Being a wet morning we drove in a closed carriage to the Palace, and were received by the Princess in the Marble Hall. Her three children were brought, in charge of an English nurse, for us to see. The present Emperor of Germany was then only a boy of four years of age. As the weather was so inclement the Princess suggested that we should make some sketches in the interior of the Palace. I made a small coloured drawing of a view looking through a long suite of reception rooms, and the Princess completed it by adding a figure. For this purpose one of her ladies-in-waiting posed as a model, wearing a similar style of dress to that

SKETCH IN POTSDAM PALACE—WITH FIGURE ADDED BY
THE EMPRESS FREDERICK OF GERMANY (1863)

(*Size* 10½ x 7½ *inches*)

the Princess herself had worn on the occasion of a ball given in commemoration of the centenary of the building of the Palace. This drawing I have carefully preserved (see Illustration).

Whilst we were at the Palace the King arrived there in great state for dinner at 3 P.M., the ladies being all in full evening dress. We had an excellent view of the whole ceremony.

During these visits the Crown Prince was most genial and friendly. He showed me his private rooms, which were furnished with the greatest simplicity. Beside the writing-table in his study was a seat in the form of a saddle, so that he sat to write as if he were on horseback. There was a large number of photographs of the Princess in his rooms, and the Prince pointed out to me the one which he considered to be the most pleasing.

We left Potsdam on the day after our last visit to the Palace, and went on to Berlin, as the Princess had requested me to attend at her palace there on the following morning. On my arrival I learnt that there had been a review of the troops by the King, at which the Princess had been present, and had become wet to the skin owing to a heavy rain. On this occasion Her Royal Highness presented me with a breakfast service of

17

Royal Berlin porcelain in blue and gold, decorated with views of the various royal palaces.

The Princess also informed me that if I went to the Royal Palace I should obtain an audience with the King. I explained that owing to my want of knowledge of the German language I was afraid I should experience a difficulty in obtaining admittance, whereupon she instructed one of her servants who understood English to accompany me. On reaching the Palace I found the place in a state of commotion. I was shown into an ante-room, where Count Hohenloe came to see me. I informed him that I had been sent by the Princess to have an audience with the King, when the Count explained that it was impossible for this to take place then, as the King was receiving all the officers who had taken part in the Review, and the Count promised that a message should be sent to me at my hotel later stating when the King would receive me. I learnt that it was the custom after a review for all the colours to be deposited in the Palace.

In the evening an official called to announce that the King had gone to Babelsberg, some little distance out of Berlin, but His Majesty would return in the morning, and that a telegram would be sent announcing the time fixed for the audience. The next morning the telegram duly arrived commanding my presence at 3.20 P.M., and requesting me to take my sketches with me. I arrived punctually, and was shown into Count Hohenloe's room. He took my drawings to the King, and shortly returned to conduct me into His Majesty's presence, and I found him looking at the sketches. The King received me very kindly, chatting affably in French, and finally gave me a commission to paint two large drawings from my sketches of Babelsberg and Potsdam palaces.

An old friend, named Blackwell, who was British Consul at Stettin on the Baltic, learning that we were in Berlin, sent us a pressing invitation to pay him a visit before returning to England. We accordingly went and stayed a few days with him. On our way home we stopped again for a short time at Berlin, where, after a great amount of trouble, we succeeded in finding Mendelssohn's grave in the Dreifaltigen Kirchhof. We placed a wreath on it, and brought away a sprig from the ivy which was growing there. This sprig we brought home with us and planted in front of our house, where it grew rapidly. Hundreds of slips from it have at various times been given to friends and admirers of the great musician, including Mendelssohn's own daughter.

Soon after our return I sent, for the acceptance of the Crown Princess, who was staying at Sandringham, a drawing made from a sketch of Lancaster, which she had seen and admired when in Germany. It was graciously accepted. Later I was summoned to Windsor to submit the sketches, made whilst I was in Germany, to the Queen, and Her Majesty was so pleased with them that she gave me a commission for drawings from several of them.

About this time, 1864, I succeeded in purchasing various cottages close to "The Firs." These I had enlarged and improved in various ways, in order to encourage morality and cleanliness amongst the labourers and to brighten up their homes. We also commenced holding small flower and vegetable shows in our grounds, to induce the cottagers to take interest in their gardens. These shows increased in size and importance each year, until the occasion became quite a gala day. All our neighbours attended, and a distribution of prizes terminated the proceedings.

A bazaar was held in Paris in this year for

the benefit of French charities, and at the request of the Duchesse d'Aumale I contributed several drawings, which, I trust, helped to increase the funds.

As we now spent most of our time at Great Missenden, and I only went up to London to teach during the season, we gave up our house in Osnaburgh Terrace, and decided for the future only to take furnished apartments as we required them. The first were at Cambridge Terrace in the following year, 1865. Afterwards we took rooms for several years in Norfolk Square.

In June George Fripp resigned the post of Secretary to the "Old Society." Several members approached me with a view to inducing me to accept the office, which, after much persuasion, I agreed to do, and at the next general meeting of the Society I was unanimously elected. I held the Secretaryship until December 1870, when I resigned the post on the same evening as Frederick Taylor gave up the Presidentship.

In the autumn of 1865 we paid another visit to Venice, accompanied by Sidney Percy. He, with his wife and children, had come to reside near to us at Great Missenden. He was a clever landscape painter in oils, of a gentle disposition and of a retiring nature. We found them very pleasant neighbours, and a friendship sprang up between the two families which continued until the death of both himself and his wife.

As cholera was raging in Italy in this year, we had to undergo two fumigations before arriving at Verona, and had to submit to it on two more occasions before reaching Venice, where I occupied most of my time in making sketches from a gondola. I found my old gondolier, Jacomo, still alive, and delighted to see me. I had employed him on each occasion since my first visit to Venice, twenty-five years previously. We returned home through Switzerland, and stayed a few days in Paris to show Percy the sights, as it was his first visit to the Continent. Owing to the war between Prussia and Austria, in the following year we then confined our travels to the north of England, and visited friends in the district.

My duties as Secretary of the Old Water-Colour Society now necessitated my paying frequent visits to town. The Queen of Denmark, accompanied by the Prince of Wales, Princess Louise, and the Grand Duchess of Mecklenberg-Strelitz, paid a visit to the Exhibition in 1868. I showed Her Majesty round the gallery, but owing to her

A STREET IN INNSBRÜÇK

(Size 18 **x** 13¾ *inches.)*

deafness, experienced much difficulty in explaining the various subjects of interest to her.

In the following year, 1868, Sir Anthony and Lady de Rothschild held an exhibition, in the grounds of their house at Halton, of the several industries carried on in the county of Bucks; it comprised lace, straw-plaiting, and various other work. Mr. Disraeli opened the Exhibition, and gave an address to about three thousand people, who had assembled. They arrived in carriages, carts, and even in canal boats. Many well-known people were present, including the Bishop of Oxford and Miss Burdett Coutts. The exhibition remained open for several days, and it was a great success.

For some years I had been very busy with my work, receiving a very large number of commissions. On one day an unknown gentleman arrived unexpectedly at "The Firs." He informed me that he was a great admirer of my drawings and asked to see some of them. He selected one of the value of sixty pounds, giving me a cheque for the amount on the spot, and took the drawing away with him after he had had luncheon with us.

In 1869 we were invited by the sister of the Marquis of Salisbury, Lady Mildred Beresford Hope, to whose daughter I had given drawing

lessons, to pay a visit at her country seat, Bedgebury,
We arrived by the same train as Professor Owen,
another guest, and had a splendid drive through
the park to the house, where a party of about
twenty was assembled, including Dr. Phelps, the
Master of Sydney Sussex College, and brother of
the famous actor. We were driven by Lady
Mildred to Bayham Abbey, where I renewed the
acquaintance of the handsome Marquis of Camden,
whose sudden death occurred shortly after the birth
of his heir. On another day most of the party
were driven in several carriages to Scotney Castle,
Mr. E. Hussey's home, where the weights of all the
guests were taken and registered in a book, kept for
the purpose as a record of their visit. During one
evening Professor Owen entertained the company
by reading from Tennyson and William Morris,
which he did splendidly. As the Sunday was wet,
in the morning we all attended service in the
private chapel, where Mr. A. J. Beresford Hope,
M.P., himself officiated as clergyman, and in the
afternoon we visited the stables. Lady Mildred
generally rode in a carriage drawn by four white
horses with postilions and an outrider, both in the
country and in town.

From about this period our tours abroad became

more frequent, and, owing to my love for sketching the picturesque buildings to be found in the quaint old towns, hardly a year passed without my wife and myself paying a visit to some part of the Continent. In 1871 we made a short trip to Germany, visiting Bonn in order to attend the Beethoven Festival, and afterwards stayed at Ems.

PASSAU.

From here we made numerous excursions to Limburg, Runkel, Weilburg, Giessen, Marburg, and other towns in the valley of the River Lahn for the purpose of making sketches.

Three years afterwards we made a more extended tour through Germany. Starting from Cologne, we went to Heidelberg, where I made a sketch of a wonderful sunset from the castle terrace. Next

18

we proceeded to Würzburg, and then to Ratisbon, where we visited the Walhalla, built by Emperor William I. for the statues of German generals. Our next stopping-place was Passau. The town was decorated with flags and garlands in commemoration of the victory of Sedan, and alive with bands, guns, and fireworks. Here we took the steamer down the Danube to Linz, the river winding in a most picturesque manner. After stopping the night at Linz we went to Salzburg, arriving on " Maria fest " day. Every one, in gala costume, was exchanging greetings, and only the peasants in their prettily quaint costumes appeared to be devout. We then turned northward and stayed at Prague and Dresden *en route* for Berlin. At the first-named city we witnessed the funeral of a general of the army, and were profoundly impressed by the performance of the Dead March in Saul by combined bands with muffled drums. Nothing could have been more solemn or grand. On arrival at our hotel in Berlin I received a telegram from the Crown Princess of Germany requesting me to call at the Palace the next afternoon. I had previously communicated to Her Royal Highness, in accordance with her request, my intention of visiting Berlin. I was most kindly received by both the Prince and

POTSDAM (1874)

(Size 10 x 6½ inches·)

Princess, who invited me to visit them at the Neues Palais at Potsdam on the following morning. I arrived at 11 A.M., and drove out with the Prince and Princess, accompanied by Count Seckendorf, on a sketching expedition, and afterwards returned to the Palace, where I had the honour of dining with them. The Princess showed me some of her paintings and sketches in oil, which were excellent. On the next morning, in accordance with their desire, I called to make my adieus. They both shook me cordially by the hand, and I must confess I felt proud of having grasped the hand of a man who had wielded the sword at Sedan.

Afterwards my wife and I proceeded on our return journey to England, stopping at Magdeburg and Halberstadt, at the suggestion of the Crown Princess, to make some more sketches in these quaint old towns.

At Christmas in the next year, 1875, the Crown Princess sent me the first part of a chromolithographic work on Potsdam, with views of the Neues Palais and the Sans Souci, good but rather strong in colour, and I much appreciated Her Royal Highness's kind remembrance of me. Later I received from the Princess the completion of the publication.

It was in this year that we were invited to stay a few days at Hampden House, the seat of the Duke of Buckinghamshire, which had been rented by the Grant Duffs. We occupied Queen Elizabeth's bedroom, which has a charming view

TURIN.

from the windows, looking down a wide glade towards Missenden. I sketched the lovely old cedars, as well as the picturesque staircase in this historic mansion. The views from it over the surrounding country are magnificent. Our host and hostess entertained us delightfully with experiences of their lives in India. I again met Count Seckendorf, who was also staying in the house. He had come to gain information in view of his approaching visit, with the Prince of Wales, to India.

In the spring of 1876 we made another visit to Italy, travelling to Rome by way of Turin, Genoa, and Pisa, stopping at each of these interesting towns whilst I made numerous sketches. At Rome we met Penry Williams and Arthur Glennie, both painters, who had settled in that city. Williams had long been a resident in Rome, as he had been there since 1827. He painted in both oil and water colours, and was for a short time an Associate of the Old Water-Colour Society. Glennie, who was a Member of the Old Society, and contributed regularly to its Exhibitions, had been in Rome for about twenty years. He lived on the sixth story of a house in Piazza Margana, and had a small garden on the roof. After staying for some time in Rome we afterwards visited Naples and Pompeii.

Our tour in the following year, 1877, was once more to lovely Venice, where I never grew tired of sketching its glorious buildings, and where we were welcomed by our old gondolier, Jacomo.

He did not recognise us at first, but suddenly exclaimed to my wife, " Ah, you are the lady who gave me this," pointing at the same time to a bright scarf which he was wearing. It had been a parting gift to him on our last visit in 1865. He was a most devoted servant, and used to attend to my wife with the greatest care during my absence whilst sketching. At Jacomo's earnest request we paid a visit to his cottage, where we found his handsome wife and her sister engaged in bead work. In the autumn of this year we made a short trip along the southern coast of Devonshire, stopping at Dartmouth, Salcombe, and Kingsbridge, where I made numerous sketches as usual.

During the years 1879 and 1880 we again visited Italy, going in the former year to Rome, and in the latter to Venice, where we were once more warmly welcomed by our old gondolier. It was during this visit I first saw steamboats plying on the Grand Canal, much to the disgust of the gondoliers, who refused to take their gondolas out of the way of them, and ran a great risk of being run down.

After having given instruction in drawing for more than fifty years, I abandoned all teaching in the year 1882, much to my regret, for it had been the means of my making lasting friendship with very many interesting families. In this year Cleopatra's Néedle was brought up the Thames, and as I had sketched the Luxor on its arrival in the Seine, I made two small drawings of the former. I presented them to Sir Erasmus Wilson as a memento of the interest which I felt in his great undertaking. He sent me a warm letter of thanks, and begged me to accept a copy of his book, *The Egypt of the Past*, in return.

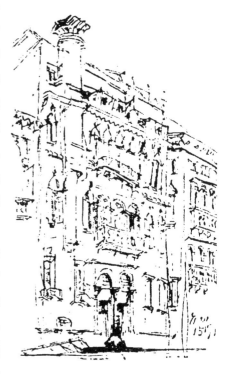

In May 1883, whilst we were staying in town, my wife, whose health had been failing for some time, complained of feeling unwell whilst lunching with some friends in Grosvenor Square,

VENICE.

and on reaching our apartments she went to bed, from which she never rose again. She was attended by Sir William Jenner and our own doctor without avail, for after lingering for a month she quietly passed away.

In the following year, feeling my loneliness insupportable, I married again, and took my new wife to Paris to show her all the old haunts of my early days.   Afterwards we went to Switzerland, where we spent a most enjoyable time amongst the exquisite scenery of the beautiful lakes.   Our return journey was made down the Rhine to Cologne, and then on to Brussels, arriving there in the midst of the municipal elections.   The citizens were so excited that at midnight the soldiers had to be called out to disperse the mob.

In succeeding years I confined my annual tours to England, and visited in succession Devon and Cornwall, the Lake district, Yorkshire, and the eastern counties.   In the year 1892, however, having now reached eighty years of age, I had a strong desire to once more visit Italy, feeling that if I were to put it off any longer I might never see that wonderful country again.   So early in April I started off with my wife on my last foreign tour to bid farewell to the many picturesque old towns which had raised so much enthusiasm within me more than half a century ago.   We crossed from Dover to Calais, and travelled all night direct to Basle.   On the next day I went to the market-place and made some sketches of the picturesque

DUNSTER CASTLE (1847)

(Size 10¼ x 14 inches)

fruit and flower stalls with umbrellas over them. From Basle we proceeded to Lucerne, Milan, and Verona, stopping at each place to make sketches. Finally we arrived at Venice and put up at our old quarters, Hotel Europa, facing the Grand Canal, where I had first stayed in 1840 and on each subsequent visit. On the evening of our arrival the hotel was serenaded by a party of singers in a gondola lit up by Chinese lanterns. Their singing was charming, and as they rowed away, followed by hundreds of other gondolas, the music became fainter and fainter until lost in the distance—a fairy scene only to be witnessed in Venice. After a fortnight of perfect enjoyment, intermingled with the pleasures of sketching, spending our days chiefly in a gondola, and visiting the Lido and the glorious shores of the Adriatic, we reluctantly left Venice, for myself at least for the last time, and proceeded to Bologna. Whilst here we witnessed a May Day meeting of Socialists. There was much disorder, and the soldiers had to be called out to suppress the mob. Fortunately a heavy storm of rain came on, which scattered the Socialists more effectually than the soldiers could have done. We next proceeded to Naples, stopping at Ancona on the way.

It is a city beautifully situated on the Adriatic, but its inhabitants are none too cleanly or honest. At Naples we stayed at an hotel delightfully situated opposite the public gardens and facing the Bay. At night the scene, with Vesuvius on one side and Posillipo on the other, and the Bay flooded with moonlight, was indescribably lovely. After a stay of a fortnight, visiting Pompeii and the Isle of Capri, and enjoying lovely drives in the neighbourhood, we left for Rome, where we revisited all the grand sights, and attended a battle of flowers in the Borghese Gardens, at which Queen Marghuerita was present. Our next halting - place was Florence, where we were present at the great festival of Corpus Christi at the Duomo. We next proceeded to Genoa, where we witnessed more cruelty to horses than in any other town in Italy, and our appeals on behalf of the dumb animals were in vain. From here we went, *viâ* Domo d' Ossola and the Simplon Pass, to Paris, stopping at Lausanne on the way. The weather in Paris was intensely hot, so that we stayed there only long enough to visit an unattractive Exhibition at the Salon, and returned home to find it so cold that we were glad of a fire.

Later years have passed uneventfully, broken

ROYAL·SOCIETY of PAINTERS IN·WATER·COLOURS 28ᵀᴴ OF·JULY·1902·TO WILLIAM·CALLOW·Eˢᵠ R·W·S·F·R·G·S

E, the President & Council of the Royal Society of Painters in Water Colours, with the unanimous approbation of all the Members tender you our most sincere congratulations on the occasion of your 90th birthday.

WE wish to mark this eventful occasion by expressing to you our cordial & grateful appreciation of your loyalty to the Society, from the year 1838, when you were elected an Associate, down to the present time Year after year, at both the Summer & Winter Exhibitions, your work was to be relied upon to grace our walls We feel deeply that our appreciation of such constancy joined to such merit can never be sufficiently expressed in words.

Ernest A Waterlow President

E. R. Hughes. Vice Pres.ᵗ
S. Alma Tadema
Arthur Melville
Sam.ˡ J. G. Evans.
Saml J Hodson

Arthur Hopkins Treasurer
J W North
John Parker
R. Thorne Waite
J. R. Weguelin.

A CONGRATULATORY ADDRESS FROM THE ROYAL SOCIETY OF PAINTERS IN WATER-COLOURS ON ATTAINING HIS NINETIETH BIRTHDAY.

only by the presentation of a congratulatory address
to me by the President and Council of the Royal
Water Colour Society on the occasion of my ninetieth birthday, and frequent visits of the President
and many of my fellow-members on my subsequent

DIETZ.

birthdays and New Year's Days. In 1907 I was
persuaded to have a "One Man's Show" at the
Leicester Galleries. It was most successful, and
resulted in my receiving many hundreds of letters
of congratulation from all parts of England. I

visited the Exhibition myself on the 26th October. It was a lovely bright morning when we left home, but after being delayed for some time by an accident on the railway, we arrived in London to find it enveloped in fog.

CAMBRAI, 1838 (*Silver*).

CAMBRAI, 1836 (*Silver*).

HEREFORD.

LIST OF PAINTINGS EXHIBITED AT THE ROYAL SOCIETY OF PAINTERS IN WATER-COLOURS

1838

Entrance to the Port of Marseilles.

Castle and Village of Montrejeau, near Bagnères de Bigorre, Pyrenees.

The Town of Vienne, on the Rhone.

The Town of Avignon, on the Rhone.

Montpellier from the Aqueduct, South of France.

Fort St. Jean and Part of the Bay, Marseilles.

The Old Bridge at Avignon, on the Rhone.

View of the Vignemale from Lac du Gaube, Upper Pyrenees.

1839

The Town of Schaffhausen, Switzerland.

Distant View of Heidelberg, with Rhine River.

Mayence on the Rhine.

The Town of Lucerne, on the Lake of the Quatre Cantons.

Lake of Geneva from the Church of St. Martin, Vevey.

Ehrenbreitstein and Coblentz from the heights of Pfaffendorf.

On the Rhine at Rhense —Castle of Marksburg in the Distance.

Rheinfels and St. Goar from Castle Katz, on the Rhine.

1840

Interior of the Port of Havre.

View of Lyons from near the Junction of the Rhone and Soane.

Lowestoft Fishing-Boats.

Tain and Tournon, on the Rhone.

149

Castle and Town of Heidelberg from the Terrace.

Rheinfels and St. Goar from St. Goarhausen, Rhine.

The Allée Blanche from Col de la Seigne, Savoy.

Lowestoft—Fishing-Boats preparing to launch.

1841

Oberwesel, on the Rhine.

Pizzo Falcone from the Villa Reale, Naples.

Naples from Porta del Carmine.

Gravedona, on the Lake Como.

The Rialto, Venice.

Mecænas' Villa and Cascatella of Tivoli.

Neapolitan Fishing-Boat —Sunrise.

Venice from the Riva degli Schiavoni.

1842

View of Como.

Naples from the Sea— Sunrise.

View from the Churchyard at Thun, Switzerland.

On the Grand Canal, Venice.

Château of Dieppe, Coast of Normandy.

In the Bay of Naples.

Granville, Coast of Normandy.

Lake of Wallenstatt, from Weser, Switzerland.

1843

Fishing-Boat off Dieppe.

Citadel at Plymouth— Mount Batten and Catwater in the Distance.

Verona from the Old Bridge.

Hospital of the Grimsel and Lake of Klensee, Switzerland.

Distant View of Exeter.

Street in Bologna, looking towards the Piazza.

Torquay, looking over Torbay.

On the Grand Canal, Venice, from the Dogana.

1844

Durham.

Santa Salute and Dogana, Venice.

Jedburgh Abbey, Scotland.

Entrance to the Port of Tréport, Coast of Normandy.

Wetterhorn and Upper Glacier, Grindelwald, Switzerland.

Street in Bologna.

Ehrenbreitstein, on the Rhine.

Edinburgh from Salisbury Crags.

1845

Cochem, on the Moselle.

Lake of Geneva from Vevey—Morning.

Old Houses at Trarbach, on the Moselle.

Houses of the Francs Bateliers and Church of St. Nicholas on the Canal of Ghent.

Vico—Bay of Naples.

Street in Calais.

The Piazza Falcone, etc., from the Quai St. Lucia at Naples.

Entrance to the Port of Havre.

1846

Street in Rotterdam, with the Church of St. Lawrence.

Castle and Town of Trarbach, on the Moselle.

Dutch Fishing-Boat at Dort.

Nieder Heimbach, on the Rhine — Bacharach in the Distance.

Cathedral of Antwerp from Rue du Port.

Rotterdam.

The Rialto, Venice.

Old Bridge at Avignon, on the Rhone.

1847

Amsterdam — Dutch Boats running in— Stiff Breeze.

Piazza del Duomo, Trent, in the Tyrol.

Casa Grimani, on the Grand Canal, Venice.

Bridge of Sighs, Venice, looking towards the Grand Canal.

Richmond Castle, Yorkshire.

Melrose Abbey from the Banks of the Tweed.

Scarborough—Sunrise.

The Pfalz with Caub and the Castle of Gutenfels, on the Rhine.

1848

Ilfracombe, from Capstone Hill, looking towards Hillsborough.
Distant View of Cologne, on the Rhine.
Water Mill on the West Lynn, Lynmouth, North Devon.
The Neu-Munster, etc., Wurzburg, Bavaria (during the Fair).
Lynmouth from the Sea, North Devon.
The Bath-Hans, on the Platz at Lucerne.
Cochem, on the Moselle.
Glacier du Rhone and the Garlingstock, Pass of Furca, Switzerland.

1849

Distant View of Monmouth.
Distant View of Melrose Abbey.
The Gronsel Merkt, Ghent.
View of Ross from the Wye
Llanthony Abbey, Monmouthshire.
An Old Street in Frankfort.
Goodrich Court — Distant View of the Castle.
Lugano, on the Lake of Lugano.
Abergavenny from the Monmouth Road.
Paris—View of the

Tuileries, Pont Royale, etc.
Old House, High Street, Tewkesbury.
Maison des Francs Bateliers at Ghent.
The Neustadt, Innsbrück.
Part of the Ruins of Raglan Castle.
West Entrance to Tintern Abbey.
Village of Cauterets, Hautes Pyrenees.
Riva dei Schiavoni, Venice.

1850

Inveraray Castle, the Seat of his Grace the Duke of Argyll.
Lucerne, Lake of the Quatre Cantons.
Bay of Arran from Lamlash Road looking towards Brodick and Goatfell.
Venice—on the Grand Canal—Palazzo Contarini, delle Belle Arti, etc.
The Tolbooth, Glasgow, from the Saltmarket.
The Trongate, Glasgow, the Tron Church, etc.
On the Chiaja, Naples.
Trent, Valley of the Adige.
The Piazzetta, Venice.
Old House in the Neustadt, Innsbrück.
Weymouth, Dorsetshire —Bill of Portland in the Distance.
Tours, on the Loire.
View of Inveraray, on Loch Pyne.

Street in Calais, looking towards the Grande Place.
Old Gateway, Great Malvern, Worcestershire.
The Butter Cross, Winchester.
Interior of the Bishop's Court, Liège.
Dutch Fishing-Boats, Amsterdam
Water Mill at Lee, North Devon.

1851

Winchester Cathedral from the Quay.
The Town and Fortress of Bellinzona, on the Ticino.
Tower on the Vrijdags Markt, Ghent.
Cauterets, Pyrenees.
Durham Cathedral from the River.
Castle and Village of Angera from Arona, Lake Maggiore.
On the Rokin Canal, Amsterdam.
The Weighing House at Amsterdam.
Rue St. Honoré, Paris, looking towards the Palais Royal.
Distant View of Lancaster from the Meadows.
The Rialto, Venice, from the Fish Market.
The Piazzetta, Venice, looking towards San Giorgio.
The Market House, Ross, on the Wye.

Remains of St. Mary's Priory, Monmouth.

The Blackfriars, Hereford.

The Trougate, Glasgow, from the Corner of the High Street.

Il Ponte della Paglia Riva dei Schiavoni, Venice.

The Pantiles, Tunbridge Wells—Morning.

Blois, on the Loire—Evening.

Old House at Berncastel, on the Moselle.

.

1852

Palazzo Barbarigo (the Residence of Titian), Venice.

Looking into the Grand Place at Lille from the Place du Theatre.

Distant View of Ross, on the Wye.

Grand Entrance to Hurstmonceaux Castle, Sussex.

Abergavenny, Monmouthshire — The Holy Mountain in the Distance.

Distant View of Naples —Early Morning.

Château d'Amboise, on the Loire.

The Belfry at Ghent, from the Marché au Grain.

The Stone Bow, High Street, Lincoln.

Part of the Cathedral, Abbeville.

Castle and Village of Mont Richard, on the

Cher, Department Loire-et-Cher.

Les Halles, Grande Place, Bruges.

Place d'Armes, Calais.

Riva dei Schiavoni, Venice.

Church of the Santa Salute, Venice, from the Belle Arti.

Maison des Francs Bateliers, Ghent.

Remains of Nether Hall, Essex.

Interior of the Port of Havre.

The Guildhall, High Street, Exeter.

Water Mill at Lee, near Ilfracombe.

Chapel of St. Jean at Orleans.

Chapel of the Holy Blood, Bruges.

1853

The Burg Strasse, Hanover.

The Rialto, Venice.

Church of San Giovanni and San Paolo with the Monument of Colleone.

Cathedral of Abbeville from the Grand Place.

Mount Blanc from Chamouny.

The Niewe Kerk on the Dam, Amsterdam.

The High Street, Lincoln.

Interior of the Court of the Wartburg, the Place of Luther's Confinement in 1521.

The Market-Place, Eisenach.

The Hôtel de Ville, Bruges.

At Malines, near the Fish Market.

The Market-Place, Padua.

Entrance to the Court of the Ducal Palace, Venice.

The Pantiles, Tunbridge Wells.

The Hôtel de Ville, Ghent.

Interior of the Port of Marseilles.

St. Mary's Hall, Coventry.

Castle of Hammerstein, from Andernach.

Frankfort-on-the-Maine.

Riva dei Schiavoni, Venice.

On the Grand Canal, Venice.

1854

Gateway of Battle Abbey, Sussex.

Basle, Switzerland, from the Bridge.

On the Grand Canal, Venice, looking towards the Foscari Palace.

Eastgate Street, Chester —Autumnal Evening.

Oberwesel, on the Rhine, with the Castle of Schomberg.

Venice.

La Place d'Armes, Lille.

Dresden from the Gardens of the Japanese Palace.

The Rath-Haus, on the Market Place, Leipzig.

Orleans.

The Ca' d' Oro de Venise from the Foot of the Rialto.

The Castle of Katz from St. Goar, on the Rhine.

Heidelberg from above the Bridge.

Old Houses in Northgate Street, Chester

Tain and Tournon, on the Rhone.

From the Ponte della Pieta, Venice.

Church of San Pietro, Como.

The Breiteweg at Magdeburg.

From the Foscari Palace, Venice.

Neapolitan Fishing-Boats.

The Fish Market, Ghent.

The Dom Platz, Frankfort.

1855

On the Grand Canal, from the Leone Bianco, Venice.

Church of St. Pierre, Caen.

Mayence, on the Rhine.

The Dom - Kirche at Würzburg from the Bridge, during the Fair.

The Old Feudal Town of Oberwesel, on the Rhine.

Castelnuovo from the Molo, Venice.

Lutheran Church at Bacharach, on the Rhine.

On the Place du Theatre, Lille.

San Giorgio, Venice.

Castle of St. Angelo, Rome.

Canal at Ghent, with the Church of St. Nicholas.

Crossing the Rialto, Venice.

Pallazzo Foscari from the Belle Arti, Venice.

The Piazza at Padua.

A Street in Verona.

The Belfry at Evreux.

Corso Francese, Milan.

Evening at Sutton Valence.

Doune Castle.

Eton College—Sunset.

Old House at Ghent.

The Market Cross at Salisbury.

Distant View at Tewkesbury.

Tell's Chapel, Lake of the Four Cantons.

Foregate Street, outside the Walls, Chester.

1856

Huy, on the Meuse.

The Santa Salute, Venice.

Old Houses on the Rhone at Geneva.

The Hôtel de Ville, Brussels.

Close Gate and Widows' College, Salisbury.

Werner's Chapel from the Inn Yard, Bacharach.

The Bear and Billet Inn, Bridge Street, Chester.

The Rialto, Venice.

Winchester.

The Markt Strasse and Rath-Haus, Hanover.

Rue St. Pierre, Caen.

Trent from the Bank of the Adige.

Bellaggio, Lago di Como.

The Trongate, Glasgow.

Ancien Port de la Ville, Bruges.

Goodrich Court, on the Wye.

Arundel Castle, Sussex.

Durham.

The Contarini Palace, Venice.

Canal Scene, Lucerne.

Ancient Manor-House near the Abbey Gate, Malvern, now removed.

Portlade, near Brighton.

The Ca' d' Oro, Venice.

1857

Double Butcher Row, Shrewsbury.

A Buckinghamshire Lane—Sunset.

On the Grand Canal, Venice.

St. Sauveur, Caen.

Venice.

Schloss Elz.

Hôtel de Ville, Lille.

The Castle at Rheinfels.

Rue de la Grosse Horloge, Rouen — Morning.

Exeter from the Meadows.

Il Ponte Rotto, Rome.

Naples.

San Giorgio, Venice.

Lynmouth, Devon.

Quai de Rosaire, Bruges.

On the Bridge at Basle.
On the Rhine at Cologne.
Piazza dei Signori, Verona.
Venice from the Dogana.
Ehrenbreitstein.
Conisboro' Castle, Yorkshire.
On the Lago Maggiore.

1858

The Piazzetta, Venice.
Antwerp—St. Paul's.
Stirling Castle from the Meadows.
Old House on the Quay at Malines.
San Giorgio, Venice.
Thun—Early Morning.
On the Old Walls of Bacharach.
The Leaning Towers of Bologna.
The Water Gate, Honfleur.
St. Margaret's Church, Gotha.
Venice.
The Kauf-Haus, Coblentz.
Rouen, from the Banks of the Seine.
The Cathedral, Chartres —Sunrise.
Verona— The Piazza delle Erbe.
Geneva.
The Keep, Castle Rising, Norfolk.
On the Adige, Verona.
The Rialto, Venice.
Brighton Beach.
Above Schaffhausen.
Castle and Town of Beaucaire, on the Rhone.

1859

Saumur, on the Loire.
Piazza Grande, Bologna.
Bolton Abbey—Sunset.
Pass of St. Gothard.
Castle and Town of Richmond, Yorkshire.
Ducal Palace, Venice— Early Morning.
Hôtel de Ville, Antwerp.
Old Bridge at Nuremberg.
Place au Change, Nantes.
Ruins of St. Benet's Abbey, near Norwich.
Rue de la Grosse Horloge, Rouen.
On the Adige, Verona.
Temple of Vesta, Tivoli.
Stolzenfels, on the Rhine.
Grand Canal, Venice.
Frankfort-on-the-Maine.

1860

Ehrenbreitstein.
Brunswick.
Place St. Pharaïlde, Ghent.
Market Day at Richmond, Yorkshire.
Venice from the Rialto —Morning.
Monmouth Castle.
Tivoli with Villa d' Este and the Cascatelle.
The Wartburg — The Scene of Luther's Imprisonment.
Autumn Afternoon (from Nature).
Il Ponte Rotto, on the Tiber, Rome.
Venice from the Dogana.
Hôtel de Ville, Calais.
Goodrich Court and Castle, on the Wye.

A Summer's Evening on the Avon, at Evesham.
The Dogana, Venice.

1861

Mont St. Michel, Normandy.
Dom Gasse, Würzburg —Fair Time.
Robin Hood's Bay, Yorkshire Coast.

I looked down on boats and barks; on masts, sails, flags; on groups of busy sailors working at the cargoes of the vessels; on wide quays strewn with bales, casks, merchandize of many kinds, on great ships, lying near at hand in stately indolence; on islands crowned with gorgeous domes and turrets, and where golden crosses glittered in the light, a-top of wondrous churches springing from the sea, going down upon the margin of the green sea, rolling on before the door and filling all the streets I came upon a place of such surpassing beauty and such grandeur that all the rest was poor and faded in comparison with its absorbing loveliness It was a great Piazza, as I thought, anchored like the rest in the deep ocean.—*An Italian Dream*, by Charles Dickens

The Rhine at St. Goar.
The Moselle at Coblenz.
Cochem, on the Moselle.
Riva dei Schiavoni, Venice.
Street in Innsbrück.
Gravedonna — Lake Como.
Martigny.
The Church of St. Michael, Ghent.
Distant View of Lincoln.
On the Inn, Innsbrück.

On the Terrace at Heidelberg.
Basle.
Looking towards the Rialto, Venice.

1862

Summer

On the Tiber, Rome.
Water Mill at Lee, North Devon.
Hastings.
The Culag Burn, Loch lnver.
Castle of Katz, on the Rhine.
Venice.
Beaugency, on the Loire.
Mill near Antwerp.
On the Old Walls at Bacharach.
Castel Grandolfo.
San Giorgio, Venice.
A Street in Evreux, Normandy.
Place St. Pierre, Caen.
Hôtel de Ville, Courtrai.
Rheinfels and Village of St. Goar.
Highland Bothies — Entrance of Glenfinlas.
Santa Maria della Salute.

Winter

Fall of East Lynn, Lynmouth.
The Grey Friars, Coventry.
Campsie Glen.
Place à Tours.
Malvern Wells.
Port of Whitby.
Sidmouth.

On the Shore, Lynmouth.
Near Loch Inver, Sutherlandshire.
From Lamlash Road, Arran.
Maison des Nantais, Nantes.
Wimbledon Common.
Holy Loch, Argyllshire.
Cottage at Malvern.
The Torrs, Ilfracombe.
From Sandsend, Whitby.
Fall of Kirkaig, Sutherlandshire.
Glen Rosa, Arran.
The Castle Rock, Linton.
The Torrs, llfracombe.
Glydock, South Wales.

1863

Summer

Midday at Haddon.
Cologne from the River.
Place St. Pharaïlde, Ghent
Sunset at Gotha.
The Ca' d' Oro, Venice.
The Campagna, with Porta San Giovanni, Rome.
Falls of the Rhine, Schaffhausen.
From the Chiaja, Naples.
Market - Place, Frankfort.
Rheinstein and Assmannshausen.
At Antwerp.
Heidelberg.
Remains of the Palace of the Dukes of Burgundy, Malines.
Arona, Lake Maggiore.
Canal Reale.
Vico, Bay of Naples.

Riva dei Schiavoni.

Winter

St. Nicolas's Priory, Great Yarmouth.
Canal Scene, Rotterdam.
Salmon Trap on the East Lynn, Lynmouth.
A Study near Missenden.
Venice.
Sidmouth, South Devon.
Lynmouth Bridge, North Devon.
Rue St. Honoré, Paris.
Bridge of Sighs, Venice.
Uncle Tom's Cabin, Folkestone Beach.

1864

Summer

Morning on Lago Maggiore.
Market-Place at Frankfort.
The Moselle Bridge at Coblentz.
Beilstein, on the Moselle.
Leaning Towers at Bologna.
Grand Canal, Venice.
Water Gate, Norwich.
Old Houses on Pride Hill, Shrewsbury.
Distant View of Namur.
Stolzenfels and Lahnstein, on the Rhine.
The Alien Priory, near Eastbourne.
Palazzo Barbarigo, Venice.
Cologne.
At Unterseen, Switzerland.
Old Gate at Rotterdam.
The Rialto, Venice.

Market Morning at Coburg.

Winter

Three Sketches, Abroad.
Old Priory at Great Yarmouth.
Interior of Richmond Church, Yorkshire, before its Restoration.
Two Studies.
Two Sketches in the Botanic Gardens, Regent's Park.
Three Sketches.
Neue Münster, Würzburg.
Four Scraps.
Three Scotch Views.
Souvenirs of Rosenau, Birthplace of H.R.H. the late Prince Consort.

1865

Summer

Beilstein, on the Moselle.
Château de Montelemart, Rhone.
On the Grand Canal, Venice.
Fishing-Boats at Naples —Early Morning.
The Citadel, Würzburg, Bavaria.
Castle and Village of Lahneck.
Inveraray with the Hill of Duniquoich.
Bacharach, on the Rhine.
Garden Scene at Versailles.
Looking towards Sutton Valence.
The Judengasse, Frankfort.

Water Mill at Lee, near Ilfracombe.
Lochgoilhead, Argyllshire.
Old House at Tewkesbury.
Pride Hill, Shrewsbury.

Winter

Two Sketches of Venice.
Isola Bella from Stresa.
Three Marine Studies.
A Mill and other Objects.
Two Views on the Rhine.
Bolton Abbey and Cottage Scene.
Three Scotch Studies.
Three Sketches on Lago Maggiore.
Four Studies.

1866

Summer

Entrance to the Gorge of Gondo, Simplon.
Lyme Regis, Dorset.
Berncastel, on the Moselle—Evening.
Venice, looking up the Grand Canal.
Lago di Como.
Bellagio, Lago di Como.
Boppart, on the Rhine.
Richmond Hill from Twickenham — Sunrise.
Arona, on the Lago Maggiore.
Canale della Posta, Venice.
On the Piazza delle Erbe, Verona.
On the Market-Place, Hanover.

Entrance to Sutton Pool, Plymouth.
Fishing-Boat off Lowestoft.
Maison des Francs Bateliers, Ghent.

Winter

1, Plymouth; 2, Amsterdam
Head of Loch Fyne.
Study at Glydock, South Wales.
1, Brighton ; 2, Study of Rocks ; 3, Dover.
1, A River Scene ; 2, Mont Dragon, on the Rhone.
1, A Water Mill ; 2, Rocky Landscape.
St. Winifred's Well, Holywell, Flintshire.
Three Sketches.
1, Dieppe ; 2, Sea Piece ; 3, A Mill.
Four Studies.

1867

Summer

Bridge Street, Chester —Morning.
Werner's Chapel, Bacharach.
Menaggio, Lago di Como.
The Courtyard at Heidelberg.
Castle and Town of Beaucaire, on the Rhone.
Bringing in Fish, Honfleur.
By the Venetian Column, Piazza delle Erbe, Verona.
The Boompjes, Rotterdam.

Street in Rouen.
Lac du Petit Trianon, Versailles.
Namur—Junction of the Sombre and Meuse.
A Water Mill.
On the Quay, Frankfort.
Entering Port.
A Storm at the Mumbles.

Winter

Recollections of the Rhine
Mount Edgcumbe and Sandgate.
Two Views of the Isle of Wight.
Three Marine Studies.
Three Sketches of Rhine Scenery.
Landscape Study.
Four Sketches.
Mountain Scenery.
Water Mill and Sea Piece.
Old Bridge — Morning Effect.
Two Landscape Studies.
Stormy Weather.

1868

Summer

Market - Place at Coburg.
The Piazza delle Erbe, Verona.
On the Riva dei Schiavoni, Venice.
Town and Fortifications of Luxembourg.
St. Pierre, Caen.
Rheinfels and St. Goar— Summer Rain.
Bacharach.

Mont Richard, on the Cher.
Tintern from the Village.
Canale della Posta, Venice.
Dutch Boat entering Port.
Granville, Coast of Normandy — Waiting for the Tide.
Old Mill in Surrey.
Orca, Lago Lugano.
Grand Canal, Venice.
Stormy Weather off Lowestoft.

Winter.

St. Cloud, from Sèvres.
Saltwood and Goodrich Castles.
Remembrances of the Rhine.
Glen Rosa, Isle of Arran.
Three Studies, Various.
Mountain Scenery.
Study at Haddon.
Mill Scene and View of Swanage.
Four Marine Studies.
Coast of Devonshire.
Lake Scene—Sunset.
The Cliffs, Freshwater.

1869

Summer

Coast Scene.
Flint Castle—Sunrise.
Isola Bella, Lago Maggiore.
Church of St. James, Antwerp.
Richmond, Yorkshire.
Piazza Corpus Domini, Turin.
Street in Frankfort.

Entrance to the Villa Carlotta, Cadenabbia.
The Rialto.
Namur, on the Sombre.
Greenwich.
Beilstein, on the Moselle.
Sunrise near Rome.

Night wanes; the vapours round the mountain curl'd Melt into morn, and light awakes the world.

Temple of Venus and Rome.
Santa Salute, Venice.
Port of Fécamp, Normandy.

Winter

Study of Trees.
Reigate.
Two Studies.
Twickenham and Eton.
Three Studies of Rhine Scenery.
Two Sea Pieces.
Three Coast Studies.
Sunset at Sea.
Fishing-Boat returning at Sunrise.
Sketches of Chester.

1870

Summer

Street in Old Trarbach
Dinant, on the Meuse.
Canale della Posta, Venice.
Fishing-Boats at Anchor in the Harbour of Granville.
Susa, North Italy.
Lausanne, Lake of Geneva.
Place de Calende, Rouen.

The Market-Place, Coburg.
The Rialto, Venice—Early Morning.
Place du Marché, Tours.
Venice.
The Chiaja, Naples.
The Piazzetta, Venice.
Cologne.
Boats running into Dieppe.
Marksburg, from Rhense, on the Rhine.

Winter

Landscape with Mill.
Raglan Castle.
Old Manor-House.
1, Torquay ; 2, Lake of Como.
Bacharach am Rhein.
Storm and Calm.
Study of Sea.
1, Peterborough ; 2, On the Tamar ; 3, South-ampton.
1, A Coast Scene ; 2, Granville ; 3, Calais.
1, Usk ; 2, Crickhowell.

1871

Summer

La Dogana, Venice.
St. Michel, Foot of Mont Cenis.
French Fishing-Boats leaving St. Valery.
Canal Scene, Rotterdam.
Rue Flamande, Bruges.
Above the Falls at Schaffhausen.
Hastings—Early Morning.
The Old Town of Trarbach, on the Moselle.

Naples from Castellamare.
King Edward Tavern, Chester.
The Vrijdags Markt, Ghent.
Posta della Lettere, Venice.
The Marché an Lion, Lisieux, Normandy.
Mont Richard, on the Cher—Summer Afternoon.
Cochem, on the Moselle.

Winter

Rain and Sunshine.
Frankfort.
Trarbach, on the Moselle.
Water Mill at Lee, North Devon.
Tintern Abbey.
The Thames near Gravesend.
Bolton Abbey.
Bodiham Castle, Kent.
Bacharach am Rhein.

1872

Summer

Street in Limburg, on the Lahn.
On the Rokin, Amsterdam
Fair Time on the Grande Place, Bruges.
At Quillebœuf, on the Seine—Sunrise.
The Four Towers, etc., Ems.
Tête de Flandres, opposite Antwerp.
Canale del Fonteco, Venice.

Scarborough from the Sands—Misty Morning.
Cathedral, etc., Limburg, on the Lahn—Summer Afternoon.
Old Buildings at Boppart, on the Rhine.
Looking into the Market-Place at Coburg.
On the Kool Quai, Antwerp.
The Judengasse, Frankfort.

Winter

A Windmill.
Sunrise and Beach Scene.
Torquay.
Rouen and Caen.
Relics at Brighton.
A Water Mill
Landing Fish on Yarmouth Beach.
Landscape Studies.
Cromer and Dunstanborough.
Going to Market.
Sunrise and Sunset.
Caistor Castle, near Yarmouth.

1873

Summer

The Ponte Rotto and Temple of Vesta, Rome.
Old Harbour at Folkestone.
A Street in Limburg, on the Lahn.
Shoreham, Sussex.
Botzen, in the Tyrol.

The Tour de l'Horloge, Evreux.
Old Gateway at Rotterdam.
Lugano from the Port.
Bacharach am Rhein.
The Old Telegraph and Tower, etc., Calais.
Conisborough Castle, near Doncaster.
The Ca' d' Oro, on the Grand Canal, Venice.
Castel d' Ovo, Naples.

Winter

Fisherman's Hut—Early Morning.
Gypsy Tents.
Sunset on the Mountains.
Near Sorrento, Naples.
A Roadside Inn and Water Mill.
Two Studies of Sea.
On the Lago Maggiore.
Yarmouth Jetty and New Brighton.
A Cottage near Malvern.
Gathering Rushes.
Two Woodland Studies.
On the Moselle.

1874

Summer

Monmouth Castle.
Fishing Boats leaving Honfleur — Early Morning.
Riva dei Schiavoni, Venice.
Landing Fish at Eastbourne.
Old Houses at Berncastel, on the Moselle.
Abbeville Cathedral from the Market-Place.

Berwick-on-the-Tweed from the Castle.
Bellagio, Lago di Como.
Ehrenbreitstein from the Moselle Bridge.
Lisieux looking towards the Transept of St. Pierre.
Verona with the Maffei Tower.
The "Golden Hirsch" Apotheke, Giessen.

Winter

On the East Lynn, Devonshire.
Coast Scene.
Barnard Castle, Yorkshire.
The Lac de Gaube, Pyrenees.
A Water Mill—Early Morning.
Cave near Genoa.
Bothy, Loch Goyle.
Mill on the Scheldt—Moonlight.
Lauterbrunnen and Staubbach.
Sunset—A Composition.

1875

Summer

Rotterdam.
Cologne — Autumn Evening.
The Grand Canal Venice.
Le Chêvet de St. Pierre, Caen.
The Castle and Town of Salzburg.
Summer Evening on the Wye at Goodrich Castle.
Tivoli with the Cascade

and Temple of the Sybil.
The Holz-Markt, Halberstadt.
Albert Durer's House at Nuremberg.
Isola Bella from Stresa, Lago Maggiore.
Rheinstein.
Waiting for Fish at St. Valery-en-Caux—Sunrise.
Coarse Weather at Gorleston Harbour.

Winter

On the Rhine.
A Water Mill.
The Source of the Thames.
Clearing the Wreck—Sunset.
At Bingen, on the Rhine.
Sheep in a Lane.
Sunset after a Storm.
Wind and Rain.
French Fishing-Boats.
A Waterfall.
Dover and Brighton in Former Days.
At Killarney—The Weir Bridge and the Castle Crag.
Raglan Castle.
Study of Sea.
A Cottage.

1876

Summer

Unter Taschenmacher and Rath-Haus, Cologne.
Entrance to Calais Harbour — Rough Weather.

. Canale della Posta, Venice.

On the Pier at Tréport, Normandy — Early Morning.

The Last Glow from the Terrace, Heidelberg.

An August Morning at Ems.

Weilburg, on the Lahn.

. The Stadthaus and Markt Platz, Hanover.

Nuremberg from a Bridge near the Trödel Markt.

Fountain at Marburg, Hesse-Cassel.

Grand Canal, Venice, looking towards the Lido—Early Morning.

A Rotterdam Canal Scene.

Luxembourg—Sunset.

Winter

Shanklin Chine, Isle of Wight.

Near Pierrefitte (Pyrenees), Cascade of Nantborrant, Switzerland.

Cottage near Sidmouth.

Beilstein, on the Moselle.

Old Houses at Trèves.

Two Views in South Devon.

Landscape—A Composition.

The Coast near Sidmouth.

Study of Coast Scenery.

Cochem, on the Moselle.

An Irish Cabin.

Dunkeld.

Botzen, in the Tyrol.

A Street in Bruges— Morning.

A Venetian Canal.

1877

Summer

Marburg, Hesse-Cassel.

Fishing - Boats waiting for the Tide, Port of Havre—Sunrise.

Entrance to the Old Part of Arona, Lago Maggiore.

The Peschiera, Genoa.

Castle and Town of Runkel, on the Lahn.

A Venetian Canal.

Loading Oranges and Lemons at Sorrento, from the Marina.

The Mercato Ruava, Florence.

Chancel of St. Sauveur, Caen.

Gateway of St. Martin's Abbey, Tours.

On the Dom-Platz at Ratisbon.

Honfleur—Calm, Early Morning.

The Ponte Vecchio, Florence.

Winter

Rheinfels and Wolfsberg, on the Moselle.

Il Diavoletto and L'Abbondanza, Florence.

A Swiss Valley.

Mountain Gorge near Pierrefitte.

Two Studies of Sea.

Ulleswater and Sea Coast.

Riva dei Schiavoni.

A Stormy Day in Scotland.

Matlock.

Mentone.

The Wye and Wharf.

A Country Lane.

A Calm Evening.

Fishing-Boats in a Squall,

A Street Scene.

1878

Summer

Ruined Mill near Dolce Acqua, Italy.

Fishing-Boats at Fécamp, Normandy — Early Morning.

Il Mercato Vecchio, Florence.

Casa Cavallino, Grand Canal, Venice.

The Old Bridge and Tower at Nuremberg.

Sunrise on the Seine at Rouen.

Ponte del Canonico, Venice.

Entrance to the Old Convent of San Gregorio, Venice.

Castle of Stolzenfels, on the Rhine.

Teatro Marcello, Rome.

Dieppe.

Market-Place at Botzen, in the Tyrol.

Canale di Barrettaria, Venice.

Place St. Pharailde, Ghent.

In the Judengasse, Frankfort.

Winter

On the Moselle.

Winchester from the Meadows.

Riva dei Schiavoni, Venice.

Autumn on the Trent.

Mussel Gathering at Lee, North Devon.
Bellagio, on Lake Como, and Isola Bella.
East Cowes; and Dunoon, on the Clyde.
Souvenirs of Loch Etive.
In the Gloaming.
A Devonshire Cottage.
A Street in Trèves.
Old Gateway on the Rhine.
River and Coast.

1879

Summer

On the Road to Rocca Bruna — Monaco in the Distance.
Canale della Posta, Venice.
Palazzo Cicogna, Venice.
Fishing-Boats off Tré-port.
Town Hall and Market-Place, Padua—Early Morning.
At the Foot of the Leaning Towers, Bologna.
Santa Lucia, Naples.
Tour de l'Horloge, Rouen.
Port of Granville, Normandy.
On the Rhine.
Castellamare, on the Quay.
San Pietro di Banchi, Genoa.

1879-80

Winter

Sunrise and Sunset—Guisachan.
Dover ; and Sandgate.

A Street in Rouen.
Scarborough from Filey Brigg.
Venice at Sunset.
On the Moselle.
Night coming on — A Study.
A Trout Stream.
A Belgian Market-Place.
Old Inn at Langen-schwalbach.
Distant View of Sher-borne, Dorset.
Reigate from the Com-mon.

1880

Summer

The Old Port of Dart-mouth.
The Market-Place, Giessen, on the Lahn.
Fishing-Boats in the Port of Granville.
S. Barnabas, Venice.
Bologna, near the Piazza S. Petronia.
Lake of Como looking towards Menaggio.
A Bit of Antiquity at Blois.
On the Ponte Vecchio, Florence.
The Mists of Early Morning at Quille-bœuf, on the Seine.
No. 2.
No. 6.
No. 3.

Winter

Stolzenfels.
Carisbrooke Castle.
Distant View of the Alps above Geneva.
On the Tiber, Rome.
The Grande Rue, Dun-kirk.

Carden, on the Moselle: The Last Gleam of Day.
Kirkstall Abbey, York-shire—Sunset.
Old Roman Houses.
Il Ponte Rotto, Rome, in 1841.
The Coast of Connemara, Ireland.
The Post Office, Venice.
Mount's Bay, Cornwall.

1881

Summer

An Oriel in Haddon Hall, Derbyshire.
Piazza dei Signori, Verona.
Town and Castle of Dolce Acqua near Bordighera.
A Canal through the Island of Murano.
Behind the Church of the Frari, Venice.
The Tour de Charle-magne, Rue de l'Echelle, Tours.
On the Canal dell' Olio, Venice.
In the Merceria, Venice.
St. Heliers, Jersey, from Elizabeth Castle.
The Great Church of St. Lawrence.
The Dom Strasse, Wurz-burg, Bavaria.
A Country Lane.
Roman Column in the Main Street of Siena.
Dinant, on the Meuse.

Winter

Study of Coast Scenery.
Grasmere, Cumberland.
Rue Flamande, Bruges.

A Garden Study.
Mill at St. Ouen, on the Seine.
Scarborough from the Sands.
Windsor from the Meadows.
Old Houses in Bridge Street, Chester.
On the Rocks in the Greta at Rokeby.
Town and Castle of Blois, on the Loire.
The Town of Carden, on the Moselle.
Shanklin Chine.

1882

Summer

A Spring Day at Florence — from San Miniato.
Fossgate Street, York.
Landing Fish at St. Valery-en-Caux, Normandy.
Tour de Mauconseil, Vienne (on the Rhone).
Ponte S. Mosé, Venice.
The Belfry at Bruges.
The Weighing House, Amsterdam.
La Porta Romana, Siena.
Near the Rialto, looking towards the Palazzo Foscari, Venice.
Piazza del Sopra Muro, Perugia.
French Steamer entering Folkestone Harbour in November.
The Palazzo Moro, Venice.

Winter

Easby Abbey, Richmond, Yorkshire.
Declining Day.

The clouds that wrapt the setting sun
When Autumn's softest gleams are ending,
Where all bright hues together run
In sweet confusion blending.

The Fish Market, Folkestone.
Albert Dürer's House at Nuremberg.
Waiting for the Boat.
Giessen, on the Lahn.
A Water Mill—Early Morning.
Two Sea Studies.
Distant View of Lyme Regis, Dorset.
Cæsar's Tower, Warwick.
Dunkeld.
Old House at Frankfort.

1883

Summer

Casa Cavallo, Venice.
Castelnuovo from the Old Port, Naples.
Canale della Posta, Venice.
Carnarvon Castle — Early Morning.
Fishing Boats off Dieppe.
Castle and Town of Heidelberg from the Banks of the Neckar.
Porta St. Andrea, Genoa.
A Street in Bologna.
Canale Barrattaria, Venice.

Greenwich Hospital.
A Street in Rouen.
The Market - Place, Abbeville.

Winter

Two Sea Views.
Off the Yorkshire Coast near Whitby.
St. Giorgio, Venice.
Windmill on the Trent.
Study of Sea.
Street in Trèves.
Boppart, on the Rhine.
Bellagio, on the Lake of Como.
Village of Rhense, on the Rhine.
Bolton Abbey ; Eggleston Abbey, Yorkshire.
Water Mill.

1884

Summer

St. Peter's Mancroft and Fish Market, Norwich.
The Piazza delle Erbe at Verona.
Entrance to the Port of Marseilles.
From the Bridge of St. Angelo, Venice.
Near the Mumbles after a Storm.
Roman Columns at San Lorenzo, Milan.
On the Market-Place at Malines.
Il Paradiso, Venice.
Folkestone Pier—Fishing-Boats going out.
Church of St. Sauveur, Caen, Normandy.
St. Peter's Street, York.

Winter

Old Bridge at Cæsar's Tower, Warwick Castle.
The Castle of Rheinfels from the North.
Waterfall—Glen Etive.
Palazzo Barberigo, Grand Canal, Venice.
Hastings Boat coming Ashore in Rough Weather.
The Devonshire Coast—Ilfracombe.
Filey Brigg—Yorkshire Coast.
Market-Place, Courtrai.
French Fishing-Boats in Harbour—Sunrise.
Old Houses at Berne.
Schooner making for Port.

1885

Summer

Canal Barataria, Venice, near the Post Office
Hastings Boats off to the Fishing Grounds.
The Drachenfels from Rolandseck, on the Rhine.
Looking up the Lake of Geneva from Vevey.
Fortress of Passau, on the Danube.
On the Quay near the Fish Market, Folkestone Harbour.
Fondamento Barbarigo, Venice.
The Rialto, Venice.
A Relic of Venetian Architecture in Padua.

Distant View of Kirkstall Abbey, Yorkshire.
A Corner in Trarbach, on the Moselle.
House of the Francs Bateliers, Ghent.

Winter

After the Storm.
Before the Storm.
The Harbour, Torquay —Early Morning.
The San Salute Grand Hotel, Venice.
On the Market-Place at Malines.
A Sunny Spot in a Garden.
Campsie Glen, Scotland.
Dover—Entrance to the Harbour.
Westminster Abbey looking into Henry VII. Chapel.
London from Holly Lodge, Highgate.
Warwick from the Meadows.
Ilfracombe from the Beach near Lantern Hill.
Hotel of the Golden Chain, Langenschwalbach.

1886

Summer

Looking into the Place des Victoires, Paris.
The Old Jetty, Great Yarmouth.
Street in Verona, near the Palazza delle Erbe.
Honfleur—Fishing-Boats entering the Harbour.

Oberlahnstein, on the Rhine, Stolzenfels in the Distance.
Palazzo Molino, Canale de la Posta, Venice.
Naples from the Chiaja—Early Morning.
Palaces on the Grand Canal near the Rialto, Venice.
Schloss Elz, near the Moselle.
Gate-House, Rotterdam.
On the Quay at Castellamare.
From the Cathedral Porch, Trent, in the Tyrol.

Winter

Fondaco de Turchi, Venice.
Canale de la Posta, Venice.
Old Houses near the Port, Dartmouth.
Castle and Town of Angera from Arona, Lago Maggiore.
Stonegate, York.
Hastings Fishing-Boat.
Entrance to the Harbour, Dover.
Water Mill on the East Lyn, Lynmouth.
Heidelberg from the Terrace—Sunset.
Mentone from the Public Garden.
On the Market-Place, Prague.

1887

Summer

The Rialto, Venice.
The Leaning Towers of Bologna.

Canal at Ghent.
Castle and Town of Cochem, on the Moselle — Autumn Afternoon.
Castle and Town of Lourdes in the Pyrenees.
Church of St. Pietro di Banchi, Genoa.
Venice Canal.
Amalfi from the Shore—A Summer's Morning.
On the Riva dei Schiavoni, Venice.
Dolce Acqua, near Bordighera.
Schmeider Gasse, Hanover.
Canale dell' Olio, Venice.

Winter

Street in Bologna.
Market-Place, Ratisbon.
On the Lago Maggiore.
Ischl, Saxon Switzerland.
Marburg, Cassel.
From near the Cathedral, Stonegate, York.
Lake of Geneva from St. Martin.
Reinhardsbrunn (the Seat of H.R.H. the late Prince Consort).
Corfu from One Gun Road.
Cauldron Snout, Yorkshire, where four Counties meet.
Venice.
St. Pierre, Caen, Normandy.
Folkestone.
From the East Cliff—Sunset.

1888

Summer

The Riva dei Schiavoni, Venice.
A Summer Evening, Sidmouth, Devonshire
In the High Street, Southampton.
The Market House, Marburg, Hesse-Cassel.
Palace of Donna Anna, Naples—Evening.
The Banks of the Rhine, Bacharach.
The Main Street, Innsbruck, Tyrol.
On the Barattina Canal, Venice.
Amsterdam.
The Market-Place, Nuremberg.
Gateway at Evesham.

Winter

Venice Canal.
Dieppe from the Sea.
Falls of the Liffey.
Bar Gate, Southampton.
Torquay—Early Morning, looking across the Bay.
On the Great Square, Coburg—Market Day.
Isola Bella, Lago Maggiore.
Fishing-Boats on the Sands, Scheviningen.
Walhalla, on the Danube.
Broadstairs — Breezy Day.
Late Evening—Murano.
Granville, Normandy.

1889

Summer

Tell's Chapel, on the Lake of Lucerne — Sunrise.
On the Grand Place, Bologna.
From the Grindecca, Venice.
Place de l'Herberie, Macon.
Fishing-Boats awaiting the Tide, Honfleur.
Rouen—A Street near the River.
Near the Campanile, Venice.
Tréport from the Shore, Normandy.
Entrance to the Grand Canal, Venice.
Near the Market, Ferrara.

Winter

Entrance to Glenfinlas.
Boppart, on the Rhine.
Canal in Venice.
Old Bridge at Nuremberg.
Hastings Fishing-Boats —Early Morning.
Entrance Gate, Hurstmonceaux.
Fishing - Boats in a Storm.
Under the Cliffs, Sidmouth, Devon.
Beilstein, on the Moselle.
Old Houses at Frankfort, near the Cathedral.

1890

Summer

On the Rokin Canal, Amsterdam.

Ehrenbreitstein and Coblentz—Sunrise.

On the Grand Canal, Venice, near the Balbi Palace.

" There is a glorious city in the sea."—Rogers's *Italy*.

Fortress and Town of Huy, on the Meuse— Early Morning.

Grand Rue, Sizieux, Normandy, with Church of St. Pierre.

Jugen Strasse, Frankfort.

Venice—Sunset.

In the Old Market, Florence.

Tréport, Normandy, from the Pier, Château d'Eu in the Distance.

Maryleport Street, Bristol — St. Peter's Church.

Winter

Farmyard, Staffordshire.

On the River, near Gravesend.

View of Schaffhausen.

St. Heliers, Jersey— Early Morning.

Distant View of Naples.

A Bit of Wimbledon.

Caistor Castle, Norfolk.

A Summer Afternoon, near Lord Somers's Park, Reigate.

Midnight Sun, North Cape (from a Sketch

by the late Robert Elweys, Esq.)

Dartmouth Castle.

Inner Courtyard, Weilburg-on-Lahn.

1891

Summer

Dieppe from the Sands.

Ancient Bridges of Rome from the Ponte Rotto.

On the Riva dei Schiavoni, Venice.

Tower of St. Rumbold, Malines, from the Market-Place.

Kool Kaei, Antwerp.

Distant View of Rouen —Early Morning.

On the Quai at Frankfort.

The Rhine at Cologne.

But thou exulting and abounding River
Making their waves a blessing as they flow
Childe Harold.

Citadel and Town of Namur, on the Meuse —Sunset.

Fishing-Boats in Ramsgate Harbour.

Winter

Stolzenfels from the Lahn.

Distant View of Worcester.

Caesar's Tower, Warwick Castle.

On the Inn, Passau.

The Grand Place, Bruges —Market Day.

Gorleston Pier, Norfolk.

Distant View of Torquay.

Arona, on the Lago Maggiore.

Two Sketches.

(1) St. Michael's Mount, Cornwall.

(2) St. Michael's Mount, Normandy.

Bolton Abbey, Yorkshire—Evening.

1892

Summer

Part of Lucerne from the Lake.

Belfry, etc., at Bruges.

Tower at Rudesheim, on the Rhine.

On the Meuse, Dinant— Fair Time.

Fishing-Boats in Ramsgate Harbour — Sunset.

Venice from St. Giorgio.

Underneath day's azure eyes Ocean's nursling Venice lies.

Bellagio, on Lake of Como—Morning.

Entrance to the Port, Fécamp, Normandy.

Church of St. Lawrence and Town Hall, Rotterdam.

Canal in Ghent, with the House of the Francs Bateliers.

Entrance to the Grand Canal, Venice—Early Morning.

Winter

Distant View of Norwich.

On the Seine at Quilleboeuf—Early Morning.

Vevey, on the Lake of Geneva.

Barnard Castle.
Andernach, on the Rhine.
Sea Piece.
On the Lake of Como.
The Castle, Lausanne.
Dutch Boats on the Scheldt at Antwerp.

1893

Summer

Blois, on the Loire—A Summer Evening.
Canal at Malines.
Ancona from the Mole.
Naples from the Strada di Posilipo.
The Harbour, Genoa.
Venice, on the Riva dei Schiavoni.
On the Adige, Verona.
Venice from Belli Arti.

A fairy City of the Heart
Rising like water columns from the sea,
Of Joy the sojourn, and of wealth the mart.
Childe Harold

Cochem, on the Moselle.
The Cathedral at Abbeville.
The Old Bridge at Avignon.

Winter

The Lake, Guisachan, N.B.
Ruins of the Teatro Marcellus, Rome.
Woodland Scenery.
Dolbadarn Castle, Llanberis.
Stormy Weather.
French Fishing-Boats, Granville Harbour.
Home from the Fishing.

Beauchamp Chapel, Warwick.
The Grand Canal, Venice—Early Morning.

1894

Summer

Château d'Amboise, on the Loire.
Rheinfels and St. Goar, on the Rhine.
Fortress and Town of Namur at the Junction of the Sambre and Meuse.
Castle of Schönburg, on the Rhine, from Oberwesel.
View in Rotterdam, and Church of St. Lawrence.
Isola Peschiera from Baveno.
Riva dei Schiavoni from the Piazzetta, Venice.
Ehrenbreitstein.
Cross on the Fischmarkt, Lucerne.
The Inner Harbour, Ramsgate — Early Morning.
On the Old Market-Place —Domo d' Ossola.

Winter

Palazzo Molino, Venice.
Ullswater.
Water Mill on the Seine.
Venice from the St. Giorgio.
Glen Etive.
Canal in Ghent.
Coast near Ilfracombe.
A Fresh Breeze.
Near the Village of Halton, Bucks.

1895

Summer

From the Foscari Palace, Grand Canal, Venice —Sunset.
On the Beach at Hastings —Sunset.
Cathedral at Antwerp.
The Grand Bateliers, Ghent—Dutch Boats clearing out with the Tide.
Old Houses at Trarbach, on the Moselle, since destroyed by Fire.
Gravedonna, Head of Lake Como.
Castle of Marksburg, on the Rhine.
The Grand Canal, Venice, from the Rialto.
Mayence, on the Rhine.
Berncastel, on the Moselle.

Winter

Weston Mill, near Leamington.
Coast at Sidmouth, Devon.
Bolt Head, looking towards Salcombe.
Gateway, Battle Abbey.
Canal near the Frari, Venice.
Naples — Early Morning.
Vietri and Salerno from the Amalfi Road.

1896

Summer

Ehrenbreitstein, Distant View of.
The Rialto, Venice.

Saumur, on the Loire.
Lyons from the Junction of the Saone and Rhone.
View of Dieppe from the Sea.
The Pfalz with Caub and Gutenfels, on the Rhine.
Tour de l'Horloge, Rouen.
The Old Weighing House, Amsterdam.
Entrance to the Grand Canal, Venice—Sunset.

Winter

At Ilfracombe, North Devon.
Castle and Town of Mont Richard, on the Cher.
Sidmouth, South Devon.
The Serpentine, Hyde Park.
On the Grand Canal, Venice.
Robin Hood's Bay, Yorkshire.

1897

Summer

Casa d' Oro, near the Rialto, Venice.
The Moselle Quai, Coblentz, with Ehrenbreitstein.
Cathedral of Beauvais, from the Market-Place.
Entrance to the Grand Canal, Venice.

White swan of cities, slumbering in thy nest,
So wonderfully built among the reeds

Of the lagoon, that fences thee and feeds,
White water-lily cradled and caressed
By ocean's streams, and from the silt and weeds
Lifting thy golden filaments and seeds
Thy sun-illumined spires, thy crown and crest '
          LONGFELLOW.

Rouen—Early Morning.
Fishing - Boats off St. Valery-en-Caux.
Entrance to the Harbour, Weymouth.
Old Houses at Cochem, on the Moselle.
Amongst the Rocks at Marazion, Cornwall.

Winter

On the Galway Coast, Ireland.
Fishing - Boats off the Heve Lights.
Coast of Cornwall.
Torquay, looking across the Bay.
The Abbey Gate, Great Malvern.
Street in Rouen.

1898

Summer

Fortress and Town of Dinant, on the Meuse.
A Summer Day on the Riva dei Schiavoni, Venice.
Palaces near the Entrance of the Grand Canal, Venice.
Entrance to the Port of Havre.
Old Houses by the River at Malines.
Old Tower on the Quai, Frankfort.

French Fishing-Boats off Dieppe.
The Old Walls and Towers, Oberwesel, Rhine—Market Day.
Portsmouth from the Sea.
Summer Evening—Beilstein, on the Moselle.

Winter

On the Tiber, near Ponte Rotto, Rome.
Campo St. Angelo, Venice.
Distant View of Mentone.
Fishing-Boats entering Dieppe Harbour.
Schneider Gasse, Hanover.
Chapelle St. Jean, Orleans.
On the Lago Maggiore.

1899

Summer

View of the Town and Lake of Lugano.
Fishing-Boats in a Calm at the Mouth of the Seine.
Distant View of Namur, on the Mense.
Ehrenbreitstein from the Moselle Bridge.
Old Houses, Bacharach, on the Rhine.
Staen Street, Bruges.
Notre Dame de Paris, from Bercy.
Fishing - Boats off St. Valery-en-Caux.
Vico, Bay of Naples.
Tragetto St. Gregorio, Venice.

Winter

Street in Abbeville.
Place in Ferrara.
Porta San Andrea, Genoa.
In a Reigate Lane.
View from Tête Noir, Switzerland.
Fishing - Boats at the Mouth of the Seine.

1900

Summer

The Harbour, Bellagio, looking up Lake Como.
Durham Cathedral, from the opposite Bank of the Wear.
Dutch Boats running into Ostend—Stormy Weather.
Andernach, on the Rhine —Early Morning.
Corner of Bacharach, near the Walls, on the Rhine.
Piazza de Frutti, Padua.
Allée Blanche and Lake Combal, from Col de la Seigne, Switzerland.
Rue de la Boucherie, Calais, with the Old Semaphore Tower.
Fishing - Boats leaving Havre.

Winter

Rue de l'Herberie, Macon.
St. Goar, looking across to Goarhausen.
Canale de la Posta, Venice.
Trarbach, on the Moselle.
Lucerne from the Lake.

Cathedral, Courtrai, Belgium.
Easby Abbey, Yorkshire.

1901

Summer

Namur, on the Meuse.
Mont Richard, on the Cher, Cher et Loir, France.
Market-Place, Lille.
Tintern Abbey (West Window).
Stirling Castle.
Fishing-Boats at Tréport, Normandy.
Wyn Haven, Rotterdam.
Venice from the Dogana.
Dymchurch, near Hythe.

Winter

Entrance to Leicester Hospital, Warwick.
Street in Trent near the Cathedral.
A Quiet Pool, Offchurch.
Dutch Boats — Rough Water.
Canale della Posta, Venice.
On the Beach, Lowestoft.

1902

Summer

On the Market-Place, Leipsic.
On the Canal della Posta, Venice.
Cochem, on the Moselle.
On the Adige, Verona.
The Rialto, Venice, from the North.
Beaugency, on the Loire.

Castel Lettere, near Castellamare.
French Fishing-Boats off Fécamp, Normandy.
Interior of the Port of Havre.

Winter

Church of St. Sauveur, Caen, Normandy.
Hastings — Fishing-Boats returning.
Old Timber Houses, Lisieux, Normandy.
At the Back of the Campanile, Venice.
Northgate Street, a Bit of Old Chester.
Distant View of Inveraray—Rainy Weather.
Cottage near Malvern.

1903

Summer

Old Houses, dated 1605 and 1617, at Traben, Moselle.
Villa d' Este and Villa of Macona, Tivoli.
The Castle of Heidelberg from above the Bridge.
Old Houses in Watergate Street, Chester.
Distant View of Goodrich Court and Castle, on the Wye.
Lake of Como from Bellagio—Sunrise.
Fishing-Boats entering the Harbour, Fécamp.
Rustic Bridge over the East Lyn.
Ruins of Marienburg, with the Winding Moselle.

Winter

Beauchamp Chapel, Warwick.
Home from Fishing.
The Avon, Salisbury.
Ruins of the Teatro Marcellus, Rome.
Woodland Scenery.
Dolbadarn Castle, Llanberis.
Stormy Weather.
French Fishing-Boats, Granville Harbour.
The Grand Canal, Venice—Early Morning.

1904

Summer

Castle and Town of Richmond, Yorkshire, from Clink Bank.
Interior of the Port, Marseilles.
Mont Blanc, Dôme du Goûte from Chamonny.
St. Valery - en - Caux, Normandy—Entrance to the Harbour.
Piazza delle Erbe, Verona.
Dutch Boats at the Quai, Antwerp.
Campanile in the Campo St. Polo, Venice.
The Rhine at Ehrenbreitstein — Early Morning.
Landing Fish at Lowestoft.
Distant View of Dieppe from the Sea.

Winter

In the Gloaming.
Melrose Abbey—

Sketched from Nature, 1843.
Distant View of Bamboro' Castle—Sketched from Nature, 1843.
A Storm on the Yorkshire Coast.
Bridge of Sighs from the Canale della Posta, Venice.
Sunset after a Storm.
Hastings Fishing-Boats.

1905

Summer

Fishing-Boats off the Coast of Normandy, near Granville.
Bolton Abbey, Yorkshire.
Hauling up a Fishing-Boat, Hastings.
The Mersey from Birkenhead — Stormy Sunset.
Fishing Quarter, Old Hastings—Sunrise.
Ruins of Llanthony Abbey — Stormy Weather.
From a Sketch at Père la Chase.
Water Mill, Lee, near Ilfracombe.
Mercato Vecchio, Florence (since demolished).
Bamboro' Castle, Northumberland.
Maison des Francs Bateliers, Ghent.

Winter

Sunset Study.
Landscape Study.

Beech Avenue, Inveraray.
Edinburgh from Salisbury Crags—Painted from Nature, 1843.
Durham—Painted from Nature, 1843.
Trarbach from Traben, on the Moselle. Painted from Nature, 1844.
Street in Innsbruck.

1906

Summer

On the Beach, Lynmouth, N. Devon.
Grey Friars Hospital, Coventry.
On the Grand Canal, Venice.
Bologna, at the Foot of the Leaning Towers.
Distant View of Inveraray Castle.
Distant View of Winchester.
French Fishing-Boats in Harbour — Low Water.
Glen Rosa, Isle of Arran.

Winter

Rialto—Foscari Palace, Venice.
Culag Burn, Lochinver.
Street in Tours, Loire.
In the Grounds of Madeley Manor, Staffordshire.
Richmond, Yorkshire.
Abbey Church, Great Malvern.
View of Worcester from the River.
The Coast, Ilfracombe.
Canal, Rotterdam.

1907

Summer

Via di Porta Borsari, Verona.
San Salute, Venice.
Street Corner in Trarbach, 1844.
Market-Place, Ratisbon, 1853.
St. Mary's Church, Richmond, before its Restoration.
Water Mill on the East Lyn from Below.
Water Mill on the East Lyn from Above.
Cathedral at Antwerp, 1844.
Street in Trarbach, 1844.
On the Grand Canal, Venice.
Distant View of Abergavenny.

Winter

Contarini Palace, Grand Canal, Venice.
Rialto, Venice.
Dover—White Cliffs of Old England, 1845.

Richmond, Yorks., from River Swale, 1843.
Rome from the Palatine Hill, 1848.
Old Houses at Chester, 1902.
Tragetto, St. Gregorio, Venice, 1880.
St. Sauveur, Caen, Normandy, 1902.
Distant View of Durham, 1843.
Old Houses near Worcester, 1848.
Hereford, 1848.
Inveraray, Border of the Lake, 1849.
Florence, from St. Miniato, 1877.

1908

Summer

Scarborough, 1842.
All Hallows, Worcester, 1848.
Verona, 1880.
Abbey Church, Great Malvern, 1848.
Near Crickhowell, 1848.

Cochem, on the Moselle, 1844.
Malvern Wells, 1848.
Richmond, 1853.
Marburg—Buildings dated 1683-1871.
Scarborough, 1842.
Cottage at Great Malvern, 1902.
Old Hall, Gainsborough, 1853.
Rotterdam, 1845.
Llanthony Abbey, 1848.
Palace Pruili, Venice, 1880.
Little Malvern, 1848.
San Salute, Venice, 1882.
Richmond, Yorkshire, 1858.
Near Huddersfield, 1862.
Worcester, 1848.

Winter

Ben Garve, Loch Assynt, 1861.
Scarborough, 1842.
Bridge of Ross, 1848.
St. Nicholas, Ghent, 1844.
Whitby, Yorks., 1851.
Venice, 1840.

OIL PAINTINGS EXHIBITED AT THE ROYAL ACADEMY

1850

Old Bridge at Nuremberg.
Fécamp in Normandy—Fishing-Boats entering the Harbour (*Water-Colour*).

1851

Canal Scene at Ghent—Church of St. Nicholas.
Broelon Toren, on the Lys at Courtrai.

1852

Porte Guillaume, Chartres.
Lucerne.

1853

Mont Richard, on the Cher, France.
Part of the Old Walls at Bacharach, on the Rhine.

1854

The Wartburg, the Place of Luther's Captivity in 1521.
Riva dei Schiavoni, Venice (*Water-Colour*).

Porta della Carta, Venice.

1855

Near the Cathedral, Frankfort.
Bridge Street, Chester.

1856

Rotterdam.

1857

The Piazza at Padua (*Water-Colour*).

1860

The Piazza at Padua.

1862

Place at Ghent, with the Birthplace of Charles V.

1864

Derby Hall, Chester.

1866

St. Mary's Priory, Monmouth.
Lympne Castle, Kent.

1867

Ford's Hospital, Coventry.

1869

Near the Market House, Ross, Herefordshire.

1870

Market-Place at Leipzig.

1872

A Bit of Antiquity, Chester.

1874

Street in Frankfort.
The Close at Salisbury, while under Repair.

1875

Entrance to the Close at Evesham.
A Street in Hanover.

1876

Market-Place at Frankfort, looking towards the Cathedral.

OIL PAINTINGS EXHIBITED AT THE
BRITISH INSTITUTION

1848

Canal Scene at Ghent—
Church of St. Nicholas.
The Bridge of Sighs,
Venice.
A Street in Frankfort,
on the Maine.
Old Houses at Trarbach,
on the Moselle.

1849

The Ponte della Paglia,
Venice.
The Kool Kaie, Antwerp.

1850

A Street in Bologna,
looking towards the
Grand Square.
The Trongate, Glasgow.

1851

Piazza delle Erbe,
Verona.
The Hôtel de Sens,
Paris.
At Frankfort.

1852

Looking up the Street
at Innsbruck from
the Golden Roof.

Old Houses in Coney
Street, York.

1853

The Town Hall of
Courtrai, Belgium.
Mill at Antwerp.

1854

Venice.
Venice.
Bacharach, on the Rhine.

1855

The Kauf-Haus on the
Mosel-Quay, Coblenz.
Market Day at Richmond, Yorkshire.

1856

High Street, Tewkesbury.
The Butter Cross, Salisbury.

1857

Tintern Abbey.
Abbeville Cathedral.

1858

The Rialto, Venice.

1859

Dover Beach in Old
Times.
Interior of the Port of
Havre.

1860

Goethe's House, Dom
Platz, Frankfort.

1861

Fish Market, Malines.
Rouen Cathedral.

1862

Rheinfels and St. Goar.

1863

Derby Hall, a Relic of
Old Chester.

1864

Hanover.

1866

Tower at Andernach, on
the Rhine.
Street in Milan.

1867

Lympne Castle, Kent.
Havre—Sunset.

INDEX

THE END

Printed by R. & R. CLARK, LIMITED, *Edinburgh.*

IN THE SAME SERIES

GEORGE MORLAND

HIS LIFE AND WORKS

By Sir WALTER GILBEY, Bart.

AND

E. D. CUMING

Containing 49 full-page reproductions in colour of the artist's best work and a reproduction of Thomas Rowlandson's water-colour drawing of George Morland

SQUARE DEMY 8vo, CLOTH, GILT TOP

Price 20s. Net

(*Post Free, Price 20s. 6d.*)

THERE is also an *Edition de Luxe*, limited to 250 copies, each copy being signed and numbered. It contains the earliest impressions of the illustrations, and the letterpress is printed on hand-made paper. Bound in white vellum cloth, gilt top.

Price 2 Guineas net. (*Post Free, Price 42s. 8d.*)

Each of these copies will be accompanied by a mounted reproduction in colour of "Gathering Sticks," in its original size, viz. 15 × 12 inches.

SOME PRESS OPINIONS

"It is far and away the best of the many books on Morland. . . . We have nothing but praise for the illustrations. The fifty pictures have been selected with excellent judgment from undoubted originals in the possession of Sir Walter Gilbey, Sir Edward Tennant, Mr. T. J. Barratt, Mr. Lockett Agnew, and others, and reproduced in colours with a fidelity to the originals which is amazing."—*The Athenæum*.

"Several first-rate books have been published on this subject of late, but none is better or more beautifully produced. . . . The reproductions of Morland's works are most exquisitely done, and are triumphs of colour-printing."—*The Globe*.

"One of the most beautiful books of the year"—*The Outlook*.

"The book is a perfect gem of its class, a treasure for artist and layman alike."—*Aberdeen Free Press*

"This admirable volume forms a valuable and important acquisition to art literature on account of the completeness of the biographical portion and the excellence and number of the illustrations."—*The Studio*.

PUBLISHED BY A. & C. BLACK, SOHO SQUARE, LONDON, W.

IN THE SAME SERIES

BIRKET FOSTER

BY

H. M. CUNDALL, I.S.O., F.S.A.

Containing 73 full-page reproductions in colour of Birket Foster's
work and numerous other illustrations

SQUARE DEMY 8vo, CLOTH, GILT TOP

Price **20s.** Net

(*Post Free, Price* **20s. 6d.**)

THERE is also an *Edition de Luxe,* limited to 500 copies,
each copy being signed and numbered. It contains the
earliest impressions of the illustrations, and the letterpress
is printed on hand-made paper. Bound in white vellum
cloth, gilt top.

    Each of these copies contains an original etching by
BIRKET FOSTER.

Price *2 Guineas net.* (*Post Free, Price 42s. 8d.*)

SOME PRESS OPINIONS

" Mr. Cundall has performed a task which should win for him the gratitude of many.
He has given us a brief and interesting life of Birket Foster, but he has done much more
than this—he has filled the volume with a large and representative selection of the pictures
of that artist, which have been beautifully produced."—*Daily News.*

" The life is beautifully told, and the pictures are simply delightful."—*Country Life.*

" This is a very valuable and well-informed record of a popular and sometimes a great
artist."—*Morning Leader.*

" Lovers of the restful old-world drawings of Birket Foster will prize this volume .
The pictures are exquisitely reproduced."—*British Weekly.*

" One of the prettiest books it has ever been our lot to handle "—*Daily Graphic.*

PUBLISHED BY

ADAM AND CHARLES BLACK, SOHO SQUARE, LONDON, W.

Lightning Source UK Ltd.
Milton Keynes UK
UKHW022057191118
332602UK00010B/537/P